John Matthias was born in 1941 in Columbus, Ohio. For many years he taught at the University of Notre Dame, but also spent long periods of time in the UK, both at Cambridge and at his wife's childhood home in Hacheston, Suffolk. He has been a Visiting Fellow in poetry at Clare Hall, Cambridge, and is now a Life Member. He continues to co-edit *Notre Dame Review*. Matthias has published some twenty-five books of poetry, translation, scholarship, and collaboration. His most recent books are *New Selected Poems*, (2004), *Kedging* (2007), *Trigons* (2010) (all verse) and *Who Was Cousin Alice? And Other Questions* (2011) (mostly prose). In 1998 Robert Archambeau edited *Word Play Place: Essays on the poetry of John Matthias*, and in 2011 Joe Francis Doerr published a second volume of essays on his work, *The Salt Companion to the Poetry of John Matthias*. *Collected Shorter Poems*, vol. 2 is the first of a projected three-volume edition from Shearsman of Matthias' complete poems.

*Also by John Matthias*

**Poetry**
*Bucyrus* (1970)
*Turns* (1975)
*Crossing* (1979)
*Bathory & Lermontov* (1980)
*Northern Summer* (1984)
*A Gathering of Ways* (1991)
*Swimming at Midnight* (1995)
*Beltane at Aphelion* (1995)
*Pages: New Poems & Cuttings* (2000)
*Working Progress, Working Title* (2002)
*Swell & Variations on the Song of Songs* (2003)
*New Selected Poems* (2004)
*Kedging* (2007)
*Trigons* (2010)

**Translations**
*Contemporary Swedish Poetry* (1980)
    (with Göran Printz-Påhlson)
*Jan Östergren: Rainmaker* (1983)
    (with Göran Printz-Påhlson)
*The Battle of Kosovo* (1987)
    (with Vladeta Vučković)
*Three-Toed Gull: Selected Poems of Jesper Svenbro* (2003)
    (with Lars-Håkan Svensson)

**Editions**
*23 Modern British Poets* (1971)
*Introducing David Jones* (1980)
*David Jones: Man and Poet* (1989)
*Selected Works of David Jones* (1992)
*Notre Dame Review: The First Ten Years* (2009)
    (with William O'Rourke)

**Essays**
*Reading Old Friends* (1992)
*Who Was Cousin Alice? and Other Questions* (2011)

# Collected Shorter Poems

## Volume 2

(1995–2011)

John Matthias

Shearsman Books

Published in the United Kingdom in 2011 by
Shearsman Books Ltd
50 Westons Hill Drive
Emersons Green
Bristol BS16 7DF

Shearsman Books Ltd Registered Office
43 Broomfield Road, 2nd Floor, Chelmsford, Essex CM1 1SY
(do not use this address for correspondence)

www.shearsman.com

ISBN 978-1-84861-180-1

Copyright © John Matthias, 1995, 2000, 2004, 2007, 2011.

The right of John Matthias to be identified as the author of this work has been asserted by him in accordance with the Copyrights, Designs and Patents Act of 1988.
All rights reserved.

# Contents

**from** *Swimming at Midnight*, *Pages* **and** *New Selected Poems*

## I

| | |
|---|---|
| Rhododendron | 13 |
| Not Having Read a Single Fairy Tale | 14 |
| Everything To Be Endured | 15 |
| While You Are Singing | 17 |
| Private Poem | 18 |
| Public Poem | 19 |
| E.P. in Crawfordsville | 20 |
| F.M.F. from Olivet | 22 |
| Horace Augustus Mandelstam Stalin | 24 |
| Into Cyrillic | 25 |
| Bogomil in Languedoc | 26 |
| The Singer of Tales | 27 |
| The Silence of Stones | 29 |
| Footnote on a Gift | 31 |
| On Rereading a Friend's First Book | 32 |
| Two in New York | 33 |
| Easter 1912 and Christmas 1929 | 34 |
| Two in Harar | 36 |
| She Maps Iraq | 39 |
| Six or So in Petersburg | 43 |
| Scherzo Trio: Three at the Villa Seurat | 45 |
| Francophiles, 1958 | 47 |
| Some Letters | 49 |

## II

| | |
|---|---|
| Dedication to a Cycle of Poems on the Pilgrim Routes | 53 |
| After Years Away | 55 |
| The Key of C Does Not Know My Biography | 58 |
| That Music is the Spur to all Licentiousness | 59 |
| Received by Angels Singing Like the Birds | 60 |
| The Flagellant | 61 |
| Master Class | 65 |
| Diminished Third | 67 |
| A Note on Barber's Adagio | 69 |
| Sadnesses: Black Seas | 70 |
| Persistent Elegy | 72 |

My Mother's Webster 73
The Singing 75
Left Hands and Wittgensteins 77
Reception 78
Unfinished 79
The Lyric Suite: Aldeburgh Festival, Snape 81
Black Dog 85
Ohio Forebears 86
Variations on the Song of Songs 91
Letter to an Unborn Grandson 92

III
Swell 101

## from *Kedging*

I *Post-Anecdotal*
Post-Anecdotal 113
Kedging 114
Hoosier Horologe 115
Corvo, Pessoa, di Camillo, et. 116
Polystylistics 117
Not Will Kempe 118
Christopher Isherwood Stands on His Head 119
Smultronstället 120
Oscar 122
Don's Drugs 125
Ned's Sister, Pete's Dad 126
Red Root's Spleen 128
Junior Brawner 130
Walking Adagio: Indoor Track 132
Late Elegy for Anthony Kerrigan 133
1969: Moon, MacDiarmid, Apollo 135
Poetics 136
Another Movie, Colonel B. 138
Little Elegy 141
A Douglas Kinsey Monotype 143
Arrangement in Gray and Black 144
Tsunami: The Animals 146
Column I, Tablet XIII 147

| | |
|---|---|
| Guy Davenport's Tables | 149 |
| Walter's House | 150 |
| The Large Iron Saucepan | 153 |
| Missing Cynouai | 155 |
| For My Last Reader | 157 |

II  *The Memoirists*     159

    1—The Grocer
        (Lorenzo da Ponte, *Memoirs*)   161
    2—The Pirate
        (Edward John Trelawny, *Records of
        Shelley, Byron and the Author*)   166
    3—The Gondolier
        (Frederick Rolfe, Baron Corvo,
        *The Desire and Pursuit of the Whole*)   171
    4—The Housekeeper
        (Céleste Albaret, *Monsieur Proust*)   176
    5—Epilogue: Four Seasons of Vladimir Dukelsky
        (Vernon Duke, *Passport to Paris*)   181

## *The HIJ and Other Poems*

I

| | |
|---|---|
| Early Evening Walk: Suffolk, Christmas 1973 | 189 |
| Frgment: At the Tomb of Henry Howard | 190 |
| Artemis, Aging | 191 |

II

| | |
|---|---|
| After Heine | 195 |
| After George Seferis | 196 |
| Other Lives | 198 |
| After Horace | 199 |
| Kolonos Hippios | 201 |
| Biblical Archaeology | 204 |
| Lorenzo England Clan Alvis Lupo XLV | 205 |
| Modernato Pizzicato | 207 |
| Their Flims | 209 |
| Family Apocrypha: A Slashed Painting . . . | 211 |
| The Baronesses | 213 |
| Asheville Out | 215 |

### III

| | |
|---|---|
| Nightmare Quatrains | 221 |
| Shostakovich Quartet #15, op. 144 | 222 |
| Parting in a College Parking Lot | 223 |
| A Winter Night | 224 |
| Vanity of Human Wishes | 226 |
| A Reunion | 228 |
| Falcon on the Alley Wall | 229 |
| Demographics: Evening News | 230 |
| When They Sent Him Back | 231 |
| Three Russian Anecdotes | 232 |
| Longs and Shorts | 233 |
| Interlinear Dialogue with GPP | 235 |
| Postcards from the Sofa | 237 |

### IV

| | |
|---|---|
| The Plumber | 243 |
| My House at 100 | 245 |
| Not Quite | 247 |
| At the Metropolitan | 248 |
| Mediation and Conversation at 2 a.m. | 249 |
| Smoking Poem | 250 |
| For an Old Actor | 252 |
| Rostropovich at Aldeburgh | 253 |
| To a Fraud Whose Work Has Come to Be Canonical | 255 |
| The Cotranslator's Dilemma | 256 |
| Jesper Svenbro: Stalin as Wolf | 259 |
| Göran Printz Påhlsson: Two Prose Poems | 261 |

### V

| | |
|---|---|
| The HIJ | 263 |

| | |
|---|---|
| Notes and Sources | 276 |

# Acknowledgments

Many of the poems in this selection first appeared in books published by Swallow Press in the US and Salt Publishing in the UK. I am grateful to David Sanders, former director of Swallow Press / Ohio University Press and to Chris Hamilton-Emery of Salt for permission to reprint poems that originally appeared in the following books: *Swimming at Midnight* (1995), *Pages: New Poems & Cuttings* (2000), *New Selected Poems* (2004), and *Kedging* (2007). New poems appearing in this book have been published by *Salmagundi*, *The Common*, *Pleiades*, *Chicago Review*, *Boulevard*, *Harvard Review*, and *Fifth Wednesday*. 'Swell' appeared first in the Momotombito chapbook series. I would also like to thank the editors of some other magazines which have published my poems regularly in the past and in which most of the pieces in this book first appeared in journals: *TriQuarterly*, *Poetry*, *Salmagundi*, *Boundary 2*, *PN Review*, and *Parnassus*.

I would particularly like to thank Michael Anania, Robert Archambeau, Joe Francis Doerr, John Peck, Vincent Sherry, Mike Smith, James Walton, Richard Berengarten, Kevin Ducey, Heather Treseler, John Wilkinson, Chris and Jen Hamilton-Emery, and Tony Frazer for close attention to, and good advice about, particular poems written along the way and/or the organization of this book.

# Part I

from
*Swimming at Midnight*,
*Pages*, and *New Selected Poems*

# Rhododendron

Several years ago, you planted
near my study window something green.
Today I notice it, not just green,

but blazing red-in-green exactly
like the rhododendron it turned out
to be when you said: *Look!*

*My rhododendron's flowering.*
As usual, I had never asked, had
never noticed, would not have

had an answer if our daughter or
her friend had said a day ago: *And that?*
*Just what is that? It's something green,*

I'd have had to say, *that your mother*
*planted there, some kind of flower*
*that hasn't flowered yet, although*

*she planted it three years ago.*
It's the word itself, I think, that's
made it flower, and your saying it.

The winter's not been easy, and the
spring's been slow. I stared at long white
papers full of emptiness and loss

as one might stare at rows of narrow
gardens full of snow. The words
have not come easily, have not come well.

Easily, you tell me, stepping through
the door: *Look! my rhododendron's*
*flowering.* . . . And it is, and it does.

# Not having read a single fairy tale

for a long long time
because my children are now grown,
I buy a book of them for the child of friends
and later get caught up in it alone
waiting nervously beside the phone
for word of an adult.

Once there was a cat
who made acquaintance of a rat.
There was a peasant once
who drove his oxen with a heavy load of wood.
An ugly fisherman lived with an ugly wife
in an ugly shack beside the heaving sea.
A man was rich, another man was poor.
A father called his children in before him.
Once there was a little girl
whose mother and father had died.
Once there was a witch.

Time passes. It is late.
Outdoors the wind is howling, and it rains.
My beard turns gray and
grows between my legs, grows
across the carpet, down the basement stairs.
The house creaks. The globe
spins off its axis, smashes on the floor.

The telephone is ringing off the hook.
My daughter is all right.

*For William, Teresa and Joe*

# Everything to be endured

you said, quoting Matthew Arnold,
*and nothing to be done.*
*No fit theme for poetry.* And I
remembered, sometime or other in school,
reading that. About *Empedocles*
*on Etna*—and then, I think, in Yeats,
who quoted it excluding Wilfred Owen from
his *Oxford Book of Modern Verse.*
You looked at me, hoping I would
understand, and yet I hadn't . . . Because
you meant your *own* poems, those
you write and show to no one, those
that lie down darkly in some bottom drawer—
those, you thought, that did no more
than imitate a passive suffering.
I should have known.

But then what's passive
when a man of eighty-five, survivor
of two cancers, sits up all night long
to face his demons in the way he always has
and sees at dawn the black rectangle
on his desk he's made of darkness
hurled at eternity in words?
This is something to be done,
endured to be everything, fit theme
for any poem. Poems in the mind,
poems in the bottom drawer,
poems heading out past Jupiter like
mental probes launched at some far sun.
They're all the same.

You wouldn't choose
to write these poems but you are chosen.
That's endurance and the doing
and the fitness all in one. Where they go
and what becomes of them you'll never know.
If you kneel down before the winter hearth
to burn them, who's to say they'll not
be etched by fire on some unheard of stone
standing somewhere in an unknown city?

*For Ernest Sandeen*

# While You Are Singing

While you are singing
who will carry your burden?
While you alone defy
the poverty of clarity?

While you encounter bitter fruit
and the sarcastic dew
while you are singing
who will carry your burden?

Travel. Sing. Defy.
Only the poem desires you
and the night reveres you.
But while you are singing

Who will carry your burden?

*Translated with Vladeta Vuckovic*
*from the Serbian of Branko Miljković*

# Private Poem

*To a friend who made a Festival and notes a time & place,
defends the 'public sphere'*

Fair and fair enough! So *not*, therefore,
in that Shelford sitting room alone,
10 September, 1973,
but on a bus, the upper deck,
somewhere between Trumpington & Cambridge
fully six months earlier
and in a goodly company of folk!
An idea's rare enough that if we're going
to credit the right person
we'd better also credit the right time & place?
Well, they've come and gone four times,
those homing birds, to and from
the singing school and slugging match,
and now, I think, you weary
of it all,
            demand the crystal clarities.

So it's like this—
            the black light that filters through
Seferis's *The Thrush*, through 1946,
through Ceri Richards' *Apple of Gower* & your poems
illuminates the private life alone
and not the 'public sphere'
however much we bellow out our lungs
in roaring, hybrid coliseums of fantasy . . .
Clichés of theory!
Panels full of reborn, earnest suffragettes!
The black light's extinguished
in the white fluorescent light of meeting hall,
committee room, symposium and seminar.
Poems erased by Poetry.
Headlights on the routine, stupefying bus
burn into the crystal darkness
of a single room.

# Public Poem

*To the same, returning home from Belgrade
with his new book, 'The Manager'*

We do not mange well! We do, however,
end our wanderings at some point
and come home. 1990
is as good a year as most;
and better, I suppose, counted out in pounds
than counted out in dinars.
But how fitting that the English now must
read your book on Thatcher's Britain
in Cyrillic! (You bring it home
with new wife and
new child.) Deciphering your codes,
grinning at your misdemeanors,
who prepared their case and sent you
into exile?

I take it back—
                       the white light that shines
from your new book, from 1989,
from wagers with the future that would wive
and father children
surely must illuminate the city & the street
however much we bitch in our bewilderment
and, alone in single rooms, disguise
the passing of our hour as black hermetic strength
and pull down all the blinds.
In Belgrade, Miljković once wrote: *While
you are singing, who will carry
your burden?* But while you carry
your burden, who will sing your song?
Those deciphering your codes,
grinning at your misdemeanors, those
who made their case & sent you
into exile.

# E.P. in Crawfordsville
*for D.D. in South Bend lecturing on*
*"Enlightenment and Christian Dissent"*

He was *en Provence* for sure
at Wabash College—
Writing there to Mary Moore
of Trenton, "Grey eyes . . ."

Writing *Cino:* "Bah! I have
sung women in three
cities . . . ," putting up an
unemployed actress,

getting fired, *Gay Cino*
*of quick laughter,*
*Cino, of the dare, the jibe.*
What, asked Possum more

than once, does Ezra Pound
believe? In light. In
light from the beginning,
in gardens of the sun—

But "Pollo Phoibee, old
tin pan," in Crawfordsville?
*Age de lumières!* Bold
Polnesi, Jefferson, Voltaire—

light inside the acorn-seed
on Zeus's aegis-day
when he'd become indeed
the lack-land Cino

having sung & sung the sun
for thirty years in
every kind of city, light
converging into one

great ball of crystal
silent as some Hoosier
Presbyterian at prayer
along the Wabash.

# F.M.F. from Olivet
*(remembering Joseph Brewer)*

Hueffer's Trade Route
didn't really pass
through Olivet, but Ford
had written anyway

to Italy: *Dear Bertran
de Struwwelpeter
y Bergerac*—remembering
the other's *Deah*

*ole Freiherr von
Bluggerwitzkoff, lately
Baron of the Sunken
Ports, etcetera*—

explaining that
a Small Producer might,
just there in Olivet, though
it was not Provence,

produce: "If it's good
enough for me it's
good enough for you,
concealed son o'

the authoress of *John
Halifax Gentleman*
though you be." His cor-
respondent queried him

re Distribution: of ideas,
of light, through a
Trade Route called
a Lino or a Monotype . . .

For investment, there
was no return: Bertran of
Rapallo from Cathay
to Bluggerwitzkoff, ripe

as Memphis cotton picked
and sorted to a pip &
woven into double-breasted
stripes in Michigan:

"Does Olivet USE my text
books? Will the clog-
dancer ANSWER a few civil
questions? Let me put

it in another form: I
do not want YOUR job,
I do not want the
JOB that you have got."

# Horace Augustus Mandelstam Stalin

A poem for The Leader, either way,
but Horace found it easier.
The widow of the Russian heard for weeks
an *Os* an *Os* an *Os*—
repeating syllable of Stalin's Ode
metamorphosed as a wasp
in the iron air of Voronezh.

Imagine Mandelstam a gentle and
official poet patronized by a patrician
like Maecenas and a friend of Caesar's.
"Octavian," he'd say.
Or: "Joseph Vissarionovich."
The syllables that trail along the poems
begotten by the Stalin Ode he tried
to write say *Os*
*Os, Os . . .*

    *wasp, axle, exile.*

Others found it easier.
*When their tongues were cut out,* wrote
Nadezhda in her book, *still*
*they praised him with their wagging stubs.*

# Into Cyrillic

I see they've written пријателбство,
but it's Greek to me. They sign
it with my name. Something's been
translated, something here is very strange.

They've written цон and метајас
and they say it isn't Greek, they say
it isn't Russian either and I see
my name. I point to Macedonia,

to Leningrad. But everything, they
tell me, points to Kosovo. Everything
they tell me points to Sarajevo too.
For example, пријателбство.

I ask them, did I write that word?
They found it in my poem. They say I stood
with Miloš Obilić in 1389: everybody
heard me shouting LAZARUS!

I tell them I was silent; if there, I stood
aside. They say I stood among
the Yugovići as in 1989 I stood between
Milosović and Karadžić.

I'm tangled in Cyrillic and I cannot
find my way. They'll help me.
They'll lead me on. I say I want to be
led out of this, away.

They say пријателбство!
The trains have all stopped running and
there is no petrol for the cars.
Everyone is shouting цон, цон, цон!

# Bogomil in Languedoc

One stone at Domazan is enough.
In southern France among
the Catharist sarcophagi beyond
a village full of tiled roofs.

He is the warrior of Radimlja and he
has come this far. He raises both his arms.
He spreads wide both enormous hands.
Although he is entirely silent here,

his mason, up from Tuscany and
proselytizing slogs along the hot Apennine,
spouted bits he'd learned from
*Interrogatio Johannis* to his missionary

friend who left the book at Carcassonne.
When all matter is to be destroyed,
the stone warrior here at Domazan
will give the sign. He will finally

drop his arms. And where he stood
the hole in space will spread until
all nothing speaks in tongues to no one.
May he, then, forever raise his hands.

# The Singer of Tales
*for Charles Simic*

I

It's a strange sound
the first time you hear it

it's a kind of moan
& the old man bows in his lap

on the one taut string
of his *gusle*

warming up as if he were a kind of
West Virginian or a

Smoky Mountain fiddler
but the blues he has to play

the sorrow he will tell goes back
six hundred years

then it was almost too much to bear
but now he sings


II

Nothing of it written down
before the 1600s

They fled from Maritsa from Kosovo
the final loss at Smederevo

and settled where they could
around Regusa in the islands

on the Adriatic coast or Herzegovina
in Bosnia the Montenegrin hills

No one saw quite what had happened yet
No one sang about it


III

Then somebody did
Sang until his song recalled

the blackbirds from the field the bones
from shallow graves the banners

from oblivion the ichor bleeding from
the wounded ikon in the monastery's corner room

Sang until his voice failed utterly to sing
and then he moaned

and then he whispered weeping
in the whispering dark air

Now it is almost too much to bear
but then he sang

# The Silence of Stones

I

In Bosnia, in Herzegovina nearby: enigmatic
standing stones proclaim
some mode of life that lost its way

upon the very field of light
where men and women danced the *kolo* once
and called to vine and lily,

wheeling sun and sickle moon, sheep and deer
and falcon: brother, sister.
Where the waters of Radimlja dry in dusty summer

enormous hands on the sarcophagi
spread their fingers wide in greeting or in admonition.
Hieratic, fetishistic.

Long before Lord Tvrtko left for Kosovo.


II

Some mode of life. Some field of light.
Before the list of Manichaean crimes
drawn up by Torquemada for the Pope in Rome,

The Pope in Avignon was heard to whisper
*Dobri Bosniani* to his agents
up from Languedoc, reminding them of speech that

*crawleth like a crab* & heretics who *creepeth in humility*
upon St. Catherine's Eve when conflagration
would consume the hills and plains, the rocks and trees,

falcons, sheep, and wild deer
of that far place already near brought down before
Lord Tvrtko left for Kosovo

where raised hands admonish or salute.


III

Admonish or salute. Some mode of life,
some field of light whereon they dance the *kolo*
holding hands, where feet tread gently

in the dust beside the dry and stony bed of the Radimlja.
On stećak, mramor, upright slab or obelisk,
40,000 hands rise up in solemn gesture of some last

refusal or compliance, join together then
beneath the wheeling sun, the sickle moon, there among
the animals and calligraphic ornament,

vine & lily, brother falcon, sister lamb or fawn,
*Dobri Bosniani* spoken for
in Avignon but silent on this silent plain

long before and after Tvrtko left for Kosovo.

# Footnote on a Gift
*for Laura*

My friend, your teacher, gives you Rilke's *Elegies*,
reminding you that Rilke lived in Prague
when he was young. You are off to Prague
and you are young, but not as young as Rilke was
when he abandoned what he later called
*a city of subordinate existences* where, perhaps,
the danger was you might wake up one sunny morning
to discover you had turned into a cockroach.
But you, Laura, are already learning Czech
and do not fear in Deutsch to find subordinate
the things of new Bohemia. May everybody thrive there!
And may you thrive there with them,
teaching English which, I hope, will help them read
computer manuals & scientific articles but not,
like German once, create a separate class of citizens.
If you are not as visionary as Rainer Maria
then you are, at least, more sane. The last thing
in the world I could imagine is that you,
with all your sensible charm, would ever want
to hug an angel rather than a human being.
You're also saner than your crazy father
who has had a dreadful year, and whose scribblings
these days sputter & meander foolishly.
He'd better, therefore, keep this short
and just say that he'll miss you.
And if you do see angels hover over Prague,
stand still and wait. They'll fly away.
You need not whisper to the city or yourself
a misconceived intransitive—*subordinate*.

# On Rereading a Friend's First Book

*You are 4000 miles away &*
*this world did not invite us.*
          —Robert Hass

These poems discussed by all the critics now
as if they had been written by a poet
dead a hundred years —

How young we were!

I see my poet in parodic costume
mumming Marshal Ky
or maybe General Westmoreland
as all of us around the burning microphone
give the finger to the war
and Stanford's Hoover Institute.
Everything was art and politics and Eros.

Everything was Eros.

Why is there nostalgia for incendiary times?
Because some Helen's at
the center of the fire. That girl in the t-shirt
and the shorts who loves your voice,
who puts your words into her mouth, who
comes back to your room when all the speeches
have been made.

I knew her too. You wrote of longing
and desire as if they could undo
the malice of the times.
You burned at night like napalm.
Now those days
are like the pyracanthas in these poems,
and we like waxwings, drunk on them.

The world looks almost to have invited us.

# Two in New York

## I  Easter 1912

His name was Frédéric Sauser his name
was Blaise Cendrars his name was Nineteen Twelve
his name was Eiffel Tower.

Only later Sonia Delaunay and Trans-Siberian Prose,
later loss of a good right arm at the Marne.
His name that day it was Pâques might have been Ray—

Ray of Gourmont that Easter and everyone gone.
Nobody liturgy nobody nun nobody
anthem or song or prelate or incense or drum.

So *dic nobis quid vidisti:* nobody nobody there
when he woke and wrote down his name
in New York it was Fear. What could he do but go home?


## II  Christmas 1929

And what could *he* do, Chien Andalou,
whose speech had the fire of flamenco guitar,
whose eyes were the gypsies of war.

Federico gracias gracias (loricated legionaries
looking like a Guardia Civil before its time,
the Harlem jazzmen blowing bagels from the bells

of saxophone and horn: *Christus natus est)*—
Feed the poor on *cante jondo,* give the weary rest.
But what could he do, Chien Andalou,

Poeta en Nueva York? Shiva looked like Ramadan.
And yet the girls were rain. He'd ransom every
singing boy he'd die for, and he'd die for it in Spain.

# Easter 1912 and Christmas 1929: Blaise Cendrars and García Lorca in New York (a second take)

What lengths what loops. In 1912 and
good enough. In 1929.
At Easter first, at Pâques. And then a good
right hand and arm blown off
the shoulder at the Battle of the Marne.
And after 1930, the Falange.
But Easter first, but Christmas next again.
A calendar, a caliper.
And One:
who'd done a juggling act with Chaplin
in the London circus once.
One: who'd hear
a violin in limousine, a xylophone in linotype.
Who'd call out *Negro Negro* to the King
of Harlem looking for the Gypsy Jesus Christ.
In 1912, in 1929.
Caruso sang Puccini & the widows in black
carried his cross through the Bronx.
Whose Red Christ or whose Black Sun split
apart like a coal? Did somebody say
*Je connais . . . Je descends*
*à grands pas vers le bas de la ville?*
Did somebody answer
with wheel and leather and hammer and oil?
*Ninguno quería ser . . .*
*Ninguno amaba las hojas, la lengua azul.*
First Cendrars in 1912. And Lorca next.
One: These three:
Chalice and orchid and book. All the Christs
all the heists in museums. Nobody
there to hear bells, nobody anthem and song,
nobody liturgy, nobody nun, nobody
prelate or drum.
So *dic nobis quid vidisti* nobody nobody
there: Encores enciper at dawn.
Ten: What tense? Who'd tell

what tensions tore the whorish times.
They're all at nines who once were six & seven.
War and crash and war once more
within the loops upon the lengths & tongs.
The Russians all wore sarafans the cats
all wore kokoshniks.
Only Andalusians barked like the dogs.
Where bankrupts dealt in a contraband *duende*
how could you dwell in the Blancos del Oro
Kingdom come where nobody came?
One: who dressed himself like a bride.
One: *que se viste de novia.*
One: who came back all alone to his room
whose bed was cold as a tomb
who had heard a hundred thousand women sing,
a hundred thousand cellos:
*Cent milles femmes, cent milles violoncelles.*
One: These Two.
Blaise Cendrars and Chien Andalou
with flamenco guitar.
In 1912 good enough in 1929.
Before the Marne before the carnage in Spain.
At Easter first, but Christmas next again.
Chalice and orchid and book.
Length and loop, anthem and gongs,
limousine xylophone linotype library songs.

# Two in Harar

    I  Sir Richard Burton, 1854

He learned Somali from the soft and plaintive voice
of Kadima who allowed him to remove the leather laces
stitching up her labia and put two fingers in.

This was anthropology, linguistics. Toplogy and trade
would come in turn. Calling himself Haji Mirza Abdullah,
he wore a silken girdle with a dirk & chewed on khat

he found sufficiently priapic that in time he'd force his
member through infibulations of the local girls
without unlacing first. Now he rose and went to work.

He'd play the Amir off against al-Haji Sharmakay
on matters touching eunuchs and the slaves.
He'd demonstrate Koranic scholarship, say *Allahu Akhbar*.

He'd mesmerize them with his tales from the *Nights*.
His exegesis of *The Sura* dazzled all the mullahs
and he wisely took a local *abban* from among the Isas.

By the southwest coast near Zayla he turned inland,
riding on a donkey with a shotgun on his knee.
Everything that was not stone was sand. Everything that

was not sun was dust and wind. His bodyguards were
Long Gulad, The Hammal, End of Time.
They sang him Belwos, fed him holcus for his colic,

millet beer and boiled barks. If the nomads took him
he would learn phallotomy, his penis gone
for scholarship among the wives in someone's tent.

Bedu lurked about his camp and hurled stones.
They called him Old Woman, Chief of Zayla, Painted Man.
They called him Turk & Priest & Pilgrim—Merchant,

Banyan, and Calamity Sent Down from God.
He gave up his disguise and forged a letter from the
Aden consul introducing him as an ambassador

and dressed up in his captain's uniform with
epaulets and sword. He marched until he saw the walls
no white man ever breached, the gate he thought

he'd walk through chanting poems. Back in Zayla
they proclaimed him dead. Back in London
Karl Marx & Tennyson sat down to read his Mecca Haj.

The Amir asked him if he'd come to buy Harar.


II ARTHUR RIMBAUD, 1886–1888

And was Harar for Sale? And were *Le Voyant's* visions
null and void? *Solde*. He'd left behind what time
nor science had acknowledged, drowned his book of magic

and returned to earth. And one must enter splendid cities
absolutely modern after all. Among the packs
of one-eyed mangy dogs. And with a taste for soil & stone.

His I was other and another still. His ear once made
him brass and like a bugle he had blown.
A scent of wood, he'd found himself a broken violin.

He did not think he knew and did not want to know
how he'd been thought into his poems.
He colored vowels no more and all of them went black.

He'd be a gun-butt now if he were wood;
if he were steel, a rail laid down in Africa for desert trains.
He studied business, engineering, crafts.

He'd sold unknown harmonic intervals for
proper calculation and would traffic
in the hides and coffee-beans and ivories of Somalia

living by the Raouf Pasha palace earning two percent
commission from Pierre Bardey on trade.
And when the Mahdi rose and dervishes advanced

through Abyssinia, he mocked Khartoum's illuminated
English Gordon, rich Egyptians & the Turks,
and took a caravan of armaments on inland from Tajoura

and was ruined. He came back to Harar and tried to run
the trading station while in Paris decadents
proclaimed a system based entirely on his Sonnet of the Vowels.

Black A, white E, red I, blue O, green U.
Was he back where he belonged? This wasn't what Parnassians
had in mind. They might proclaim King Menelek

himself a symbolist if he became Negasti & Hararis were
his businessmen of Empire up and down their narrow streets.
There was no Amir left in town, no Wazir.

Sultan Ahmad bin Sultan Abibakr had asked Captain Burton
if he'd come to buy Harar. The poet advertised the sale
of priceless bodies, *hors de toute race, hors de tout monde*.

Travelers would not render their commission for a while.

## She Maps Iraq

She maps Iraq. For England and for Empire
and the Man Who Would Be King.
She is Miss Gertrude Bell, a friend of T.E.L.
and Faisal. She knows much more

than all the men around her table, and she knows
they know this and despise her for her
knowledge and her fluent Arabic. They need her though,
and so she maps Iraq. They cannot find

a thing: no well or wall or wildflower blooming
where they all think nothing blooms.
What they know they only say to one another
at their club—*conceited silly flatchest windbag daughter*

*of the Ironworks Bell & Bell.* They'd all
sweat their smelting jealousies in Turkish baths.
She maps Iraq. They all take notes. They lean across
her table, light her endless cigarettes.

She was in love with Doughty-Wylie, Charles Doughty's
nephew who could quote in Persian poetry
that she translated back in 1893 with her lost Cadogan—
*Songs of dying laughter, songs of love once warm.*

Churchill sent D-Wylie to Gallipoli to die a hero and so now
she maps Iraq for Churchill, too. *And still a graver
music runs beneath the tender love notes of
those songs* she murmurs to herself, her pencil poised.

She'd loved dear old Cadogan, too, but Hugh
the foundry magnate Bell opposed a marriage with this man
of so few prospects, and she loved her brilliant father
most of all. (The gossips had her now in love with Faisal.)

At tea with Mrs. Humphrey Ward or Jenny Lind
or Henry James she used to say: *I know your work,* and
*I shall go to Oxford.* At Balliol, she was obliged
to sit in lectures on the history of Empire with her back

to tutor Mr. Black, and yet she got a First in spite of that,
and now she maps Iraq. There was ancient Hit
where Babylonians found oil to light their lamps. And here
was Ukhaidir, her own discovery & gift to archaeology,

or so she hoped, in photographs & sketches, measurements
of every kind. They wrote down in their notes *Petroleum at Hit*
and made no reference to the ruins at Ukhaidir.
*Arabia Deserta* was beside her even now, whispering

archaic Englishes that Doughty drew from Spenser,
whispering his nephew's name. She'd lead a gift-mare through
the very room and not a single hand would offer her
a sheep's eye or a carpet full of pillows on the desert sand.

She maps Iraq. She thinks their nodding heads resemble camels'
and she almost laughs remembering just yesterday
when Churchill slid from his high saddle on a camel's hump
in front of Lawrence & the Sphinx. She says that Baghdad,

Bosrah, Mosul should be *vilayets* but unified by the Sharif
the French drove out of Syria—the French, whose
archaeologists wrote up her finds at Ukhaidir before she
published *Amurath to Amurath.* The camels' heads nod on.

She says and here is Carchemish where all the Hittites
watched through their binoculars as Germans
built the Baghdad railway bridge. Had they visited
Assyrians in Kalat Shergat, all the Jewish tribes there in Haran?

She'd wager none of them had been detained by the Rashids
but she was in a harem at Hayil back when Ibn Saud marched
that way before the war. She wonders now how many of
those pills she took. Lawrence would be difficult for wives

of all these men, but she herself was thought to be impossible.
Doughty-Wiley had a wife, and so did Cox, and even
Faisal, although no one ever saw her. They said her own visits
to the sheiks were scandalous where she was treated

as an honorary man. She smoked with them and drank their
bitter coffee and could gallop their best horses
with their favorite sons. Here were twelve oases and
the routes to them and these were villages one shouldn't

for a moment underestimate. Faisal held her once so long
she felt she couldn't breathe, but then he only kissed her hand.
She still read Doughty-Wiley's letters in the night.
But where exactly draw these lines demarking Syria and

Palestine Iraq Arabia & Jordan Britain & the French had made
agreements while the Zionists had wondered was she Arab
or an English woman in her Bond Street skirts and funny hats.
It made her very tired. They said her influence had waned

but gave her titles both officially and otherwise: It was perhaps
too many of those pills she took to sleep.
She maps Iraq, but cannot now recall if in her wild travels
she had seen what she had said: *I know your work*, and

*I shall go to Oxford.* She was Oriental Secretary and she had
an O.B.E. She was Director of Antiquities in Baghdad
at her own museum. *And still a graver music runs beneath
the tender love notes of those songs* did not translate

Petroleum at all. She's feeling very thirsty now for water
and not oil, speaks to them of dizziness, a spell, some word
you don't pronounce as it is written or a place you've
never been that seems to be familiar as your English home.

The men stand up around her map and someone says
*It isn't here* and she says *but I've told you that was lost.*
Everybody leaves. They pluck their camels' heads
right off their shoulders as they go and she is back at Balliol

or in her bed and *Who said anything about Americans*
she'd give this land to Fattuh, her dear servant, or to Hugh,
her father, and you see there on her map Northumbria
is clearly inidcated as a corner of this world.

She longs for sleep in which her map would gather her
into its folds and roll her up as in a carpet taken
from the desert floor. Daughter of a foundry, she has been
a maid of Iron. For she has mapped Iraq . . .

whispers only . . . *Faisal, Fattuh, Father, take me back.*

# Six or So in Petersburg

They go out to the theatre. It's Lermontov, his Masquerade.
Shostakovich might have made an opera of it
if they hadn't executed Meyerhold. But that comes later on.
Tonight it's Meyerhold's production, it is Petersburg,
it is no ordinary evening in October. Everybody's there.

Everybody who is anyone is there. Anna Andreyevna
only managed tickets for the dress rehearsal; she isn't
anybody who is anyone just yet. The beautiful Gorenka.
When she bites her tongue she tastes her Tartar blood.
She leaves a dress shop on the afternoon it all begins.

It all begins like theatre, like Masquerade, like Lermontov.
It all begins like Meyerhold. Perhaps those mummers
mime it all, perhaps the bodies lying in the street are only
doused with buckets of red paint. The painters all come too.
The painters and the dancers and the violinists mime.

All the dead men get back up to much applause.
All the dead men lie there in the streets. Either way
the beautiful Gorenka tastes her Tartar blood & speaks.
She makes a music of this Meyerhold, this Masquerade.
The lovesick Gumilyov tells her he is dead, a suicide.

Gumilyov is not dead, he only mimes. He's shot, of course,
but that comes later on. He is in Paris, not in Petersburg.
It's Knyazev who has killed himself for love. Who will die
for Vladimir Ulyanov? Everyone who goes to Masquerade.
Gorenka has become Akhmatova. She'll write it down.

They write down everything you say. The ones who ask
you where you live, who ask your name, who ask you
why you're playing in this Masquerade. Gumilyov rides his
wayward tram back home. He cannot tell the severed heads
from cabbages with heads so cheap on sale in every shop.

They come out of the theatre and stare at all the fires.
Petersburg is burning down. It is revised, with major cuts
provided by the censors. That is, the novel by Bely.
That is, his *Petersberg*. Nikolai Apollonovich stands before
his mirror as a blood-red domino in an assassin's mask:

His hand upon a bust of Kant. The mummers in the poem
by Anna Andreyevna mime another age on the Fontanka.
She conjurs there a guest come from the future bringing doom
instead of flowers; she writes upon the writings of the dead.
There's Mandelstam; there's Meyerhold; there's Blok.

On the obverse, Pushkin's whispering *Your future is your past;
Drink the waters of Lethe.* And in her other ear the Engineer
of Souls: *Then tell us who is who and who's alive and who
is dead; we'll melt your tripple-bottomed black libretto down into
a hymn of state and gift you with a row of dots out of Onegin.*

. . .

Shostakovich plays a movement from his Seventh as the shells
explode outside his flat. He wraps himself in Gogol's overcoat
and waits for the evacuation to begin. The painters will come too.
Someone must be there to pour the blood. Beneath the window
Peter on his high bronze horse pursues the fleeing mad Evgeny.

# Scherzo Trio: Three at the Villa Seurat

I Henry

I say fuck fuck fuck fuck fuck
in all my books.
Women I call cunts and men
except for Larry all are assholes.

Eliot declares that I'm a genius
but refuses all my books at Faber.
*Cancer, Capricorn, Black Spring,*
you get them cheap from Obelisk.

Fuck fuck fuck fuck fuck.
You read it there in all my books:
that women all are cunts and men
except for Larry all are assholes.


II Larry

I write heraldic prose and someone
hits upon Baroque in a review.
But I don't like Baroque; I like
bouzouki music, I like Corfu.

I'd screw Anaïs like the rest of them
if she would let me in. Why am I
the only one who doesn't get it?
I said to Henry when I met him,

You're the only one with fever'd
brain enough to see the only way
for art to go today
is straight on down the sewer!

### III Anaïs

I'm delicate, incestuous, incessant
and insane. I sleep with
all my shrinks and none of them at all
are like my famous father.

Henry's only good for once a week
but that's a great improvement on Artaud.
My diary is better than the books
by all these crooks: They will be mine forever

when all their pages have been pulped.
Fashion is as fickle as a feather.
I do say clever things. Call me from my nap
if Edmund Wilson ever rings.

# Francophiles, 1958

*La transhumance du Verbe,* incanted René Char.
And so we would repasture
in the tower-room and try to think in French
directed by a *berger* from Morocco. Frogs were in.
Brits and Yanks were out. Hell was other people
we'd proclaim, pointing out each other's *mauvaise foi.*
What was not absurd was certainly surreal, essence rushing
headlong at existence all the way from Paris to
Vauclouse. Over hills we sent our sheep with Cathar heretics—
through unsettled valleys into settled code. (One day
predatory age would eat our lambs, but that was
too far off to see): We went to bed with both Bardot
and de Beauvoir. Fantastic volunteers of *Le Maquis,* we
knew about Algeria, about
Dien Bien Phu . . .
                        Camus was in,
Steinbeck clearly out.
Sartre had overestimated novels by Dos Pasos.
Pesos paid the wage of Sisyphus to roll
his boulder up the hill;
dollars went a good long way on continental holidays
if you could catch the Maître's mistress
mouthing his enciphered wholly unacknowledged
fully legislative & heraldic letter: *d'* . . .

But SOE and FLN were not on anybody's SATs.
No trees blossomed into *Hypnos Leaves.*
No one gave us arms.
No one's army occupied our town, and not
a single paratrooper dangled in his harness from our tower.
Camus declared in Stockholm: *I'm no existentialist.*
*But if obliged to choose between the works*
*of Justice and ma mère, I will choose ma mère.*
That surprised us as we greedily
claimed Justice for our own—which was easy
with our mothers safe at home & cooking us authentic dinners
that we ate like old conspirators in jails.

Still, the poet transcribed secret words
directly in his poems.
They named the roads, the villages, coordinates for
sabotage, assassination, unforeseen attacks.
We heard a beeping in the wires, the bleating
of a little flock, a change of key in those reiterations
by Ravel when music, like the Word,
tumbles starving into green transhumant fields.

# Some Letters

In the end it was his daughter who would write
the book about his mother, but Wayland
fended off biographers for years after academics
on the trail of Robert Falcon Scott

trashed her on their way to the pole. It was 1980
and I lived that year at Clare Hall in Cambridge
with my wife, half-sister of Liz, wife of Wayland Young,
Lord Kennet. Wayland had been Hilton-Young at first,

like his father, Lady Scott's second husband, but he
scrapped the Hilton part when he joined the Labour Party
(at the same time, about, that Wedgwood-Benn had
smashed the Wedgwood saying, You can call me Tony).

Anyway, Wayland phoned one day and asked if I
would go identify myself at the U.L. archive and bring him
something to The Lacket, a small cottage in Wiltshire where
Lytton Strachey had written *Eminent Victorians*, I think,

sometime after Wayland's father, the first Lord Kennet,
had proposed to, and been refused by, Virginia Woolf.
He wanted the letters, deposited by him on extended loan,
that T.E. Lawrence wrote to Lady Scott after she became

a Hilton-Young and T.E.L. became a Ross, and then a Shaw.
Or was it Shaw, and afterwards Ross? I showed them my ID,
an Indiana driver's license, and they gave me a large envelope
with all the letters. I said, Can I just walk out with these?

The librarian said I could, being "Lord Kennet's representative."
So I took them to the station and caught a train for
Wiltshire, reading in astonishment Lawrence's account to
Wayland's mother, then a sculptress keen to do his bust,

about his changes in identity and habits. At one stop I got out,
Xeroxed all the letters, and caught another train.
Lawrence of Arabia! Or Shaw. Or Ross. He wrote to
Wayland's mother: "T.E. Lawrence is no more."

Wayland's mother, too, had changed from the days
when Scott would dine with her at luncheon parties that
included Barrie, Beerbohm, Isadora Duncan, Gertrude Stein.
(Peter Scott, Wayland's half-brother, had been named

for Peter Pan, a work written not in Wiltshire at the Lacket
but at Wayland's London house on Bayswater Rd.
You may have seen the blue historic plaque affixed above the door.)
When I got to the Lacket, Wayland told me that another biographer

had been in touch and that he'd grown wary, thought he'd
better see what T.E.L. had written before granting access
to the file. I gave him the originals and sat there having tea
and thinking about Lawrence, Scott, Strachey, Barrie, Beerbohm

and Virginia Woolf. After a while, Wayland leaned over
and passed me something—my driver's license, it appeared, had
been slipped by the archivist in among the letters.
Our eyes met for a moment, and I suddenly remembered all

those photocopies I had made coming down. Better burn those.
But I smiled and took the Indiana License, another cup of tea,
a scone with marmalade, and said: Lawrence of Arabia! Good Lord!
And Wayland said: Yes. A very strange little man.

II

# Dedication to a Cycle of Poems on the Pilgrim Routes to Santiago de Compostela

And this is for my daughter, who,
in the middle of the map I try to draw, the making,
struggles to a Compostela of her own

in pain & torment. *What did I do wrong?* she asks.
*What did I do wrong
to suffer this?*—The primal, secret, terrified & universal

query of the sick. She did nothing wrong.
And yet she walks in chains
along a Lemosina or a Tolosona Dolorosa

winding through uncertainty & grief
to disappear into unknowable remote far distances.
She walks ahead of me, doubting that

I follow, although I call out loudly & I try,
But also, when she herself must rest, unable to go on,
at hospital or hospice on the way, then

I'll learn to wait, a patient too, without impatience.
Perhaps we'll see pass by every single other living soul!
The routes were arduous, each one,

and cemeteries in the churchyards far outnumber
monuments recording cures miraculous
achieved along the way. You had to get there somehow.

You had to show the saint your poor
tormented frail human body. You had to drag it there
driven by your guilt or your desire.

The journey's so entirely strange I cannot fathom it.
And yet this map, this prayer:
That she will somehow get to Compostela,

take that how you may, & that I will be allowed to follow.
And that Santiago, call him what you like,
Son of Thunder, Good Saint Jacques, The Fisherman,

Or whoever really lies there—
hermit, heretic, shaman healer with no name—
will somehow make us whole.

# After Years Away

### I — My Bed, My Father's Bell

First my bed, then his, now mine again—
just for a week.

He died in it, my father, where for years
I'd lie beside my pretty love,

alive and indiscreet.
He moved in here so she, my mother,

might sleep undisturbed while he gazed darkly
all night long into the dark.

In need, he'd ring a small brass bell
molded in the shape

of a hoop-skirted lady
sweeping with a broom and looking grim.

I see it now,
lying sideways on a row of books.

He'd ring it and she'd come to him.


### II — My Father's Bell, My Grandfather's Books

The books are remnants of a city gardener's
life: the works of Emerson,

a Tennyson collected, *Paradise Lost*.
He's written in his Milton

*1650*
*1608*

*42 years.* And on the title page:
*Begun in January, 1893, and never finished.*

In another hand: *Happy new year to you, 1892.*
He's figured that J.M. was 42 in 1650

when he wrote his answer to Salmasius
and lost his sight.

*Defensio pro Populo Anglicano.*
At the Presbyterian funeral a cousin

asked: *are you religious?* and I said
in callow family disaffection:

*Gnostic. Bogomil. Albigensian for heaven's sake.*
On the *Ex Libris* plate:

*Poetry. This book will not be loaned.*
And underneath: *couldn't dig this month.*

*Ground as cold as hell.*
I replace the book. I pick up the bell.


III — My Mother's Broom, My Father's Bell

My mother stashed those books in here
for me to find. My father

would have seen them, reaching for his bell,
but they were not for him.

She left them here, her father's only legacy,
as she began to sweep.

She swept the hearth, the porch and drive,
she even swept the street.

(She swept my father once entirely
off his feet.)

While he lay dying & while I sat reading books,
she swept his mortal breath away,

I think.
When she heard the ringing here . . .

And then swept circles round & round the bier
as I said *Gnostic, Bogomil.*

Although the ground was cold as hell
they dug the grave & dug it deep.

Sweet sleep. Sweep sweep.
There's no one here to listen or to care,

and so I ring the bell—
creating great commotion *there.*

# The Key of C Does Not Know My Biography
*(Stravinsky, 1937–1942)*

In Sancellemoz they read the *Philokalia* while
in the rue St. Honoré his *moderato alla breve* coughed
not once for Nicodemus on Mount Athos or
Makarius of Corinth even if the resurrection were Docetic
and the tonic a familiar C.
It was the worst year of his life.
Tuberculosis drowned his daughter Mika and
his wife at Sancellemoz; he himself and then Milena
spat up blood; his mother died
and Wehrmacht panzers rumbled toward the Maginot.
He wrote in C. He wrote *Larghetto concertante*
in the sanatorium and though it was no *Sacre du Printemps*
the spring would have its rites: fists of earth
thrown in open graves at Saint Geneviève.
He wrote in C in C in C, was diatonic in extreme
and in the suite of dances the fugatos
the Italianate transparency of theme you'd never
guess he lit the candles every night in agony
beside the image of *La Vierge du perpétuel secours*.

Then Hollywood. Then the *allegretto* and the *largo*
and the Disney dinosaurs roaring to Stokowski's *Sacre*
that frightened little children at the matinees.
Then war. Then holocaust. He wrote in C.
His one entirely boring work had saved his life
by counting repetitions like the telling of a rosary—
dominant and tonic, tonic and the dominant—
tonal bricks to build a house in which he'd pitch at last
a tall dodecaphonic tent and
call the Angel down for Abraham.
He said the key of C
did not know his biography.

# That Music is the Spur to all Licentiousness
*(Janáček in love)*

The little birds would flutter to
his Katya's grave his Kyrie in Glagolitic
sing out lustily a *Gaspodi pomiluj.*
*Salva!* (Gloria!)
                      But *non credo in Signeur Dieu by god*
whispered every violin he heard
some gypsy Dorian raised fourth cantabile his word consumed &
sounding out *nápěvky* Ka-mi-la. Half his age
and twice his muse she'd be his Katya his Kabanová
his lesson to Renard & Reineke
on how to chase a fox in old Moravia. *Bystrouška!*

Still those two quartets would feed on crazy
Tolstoy fed on *Kreutzer* weeping presto by the moonlit
porch at Yasnaya Polyana: Tender Lyovochka all
undone and fucking Sonia in the nave of his own *niet*
a Pozdnychev strung out in Prague *sul ponticello.*
That music is the spur to all licentiousness
the maestro doubts. His love unconsummated he embraces
only sound. And it dissolves.
And when the Angel asks him would he
make his peace with God the dying Janáček replies
but what is peace
and what is would
and what is God Janáčková.

# Received by Angels Singing Like the Birds
*(Messiaen, 1992)*

*Venite . . . inginocchiatevi &*
Susanna's answered
by a Garden Warbler and a Kakapo.
*Figaro!* Strings, cymbal, wind machine, les ondes—
those bells bells from Assisi.
L'Ange Voyageur steps from Fra Angelico's *Annunciation*
with his wings unfurled, his feathers
quinticolored red & yellow, blue & green & mauve,
and sings: *Cantico della creature cantico*
glissando Gerygone percussion tuned a new
Noh-Caledonian: *What is your name?*
*Ondeolivier avec offrandes pas oubliées.*
And suddenly a dawn sky of Skylarks. Orioles
and Lyrebirds, suddenly antiphony
of Icterine and Thrush. Semitone descent from A
as demisemiquaver . . . then
arpeggio of cloud,
tremolo among the shining shaken leaves.

*For Kym*

# The Flagellant *(i.m. Percy Grainger)*

1.

Italian wouldn't do at all
to tell his band the way they ought to feel
when they played the score.

*Bundle it & jogtrot through these bars,* he'd say:
*Lower notes of woggle well to the fore.*
*Easy goes but cling it, louden lots!*

He'd have them lay on with a will.
He'd play the flageolet.
Some there were who'd find his ways flagitious.


2.

Melbourne in the mornings of
a mother's love:—His pregnant Rose would
gaze upon Apollo's alabaster

on her dresser, pray that he be gifted with
the sinlessness of song, and hang
the horsewhip by the empty music stand.

This son of sunlight might just winch it
short of woggle, jogtrot where he ought to cling,
bungle where the lauding rose at dawn.


3.

Carried by that praise well round the world,
Mother's "Bubbles," now her "Perks," yammered
in his made up lingo to the friends who'd listen

while he stood up naked on the lid of his piano
talking Maori Swedish German & Icelandic
all at once and lecturing the Frankfurt musicologists

on Kipling. His *Marching Song* would be performed
by whistling girls tramping through the open air
in broken strides at who/4 what/4 & in double Dutch.


4.

The *Shorter Music Dictionary* (Willi Apel, Harvard)
has no listing for *Brigg Fair*. There's no mention
there that in 1900 PG wrote a Sea Song which required

a band of winds to play at 7/35 and 9/17. Between
the *Frauenliebe* songs and *Freischütz, Der*
you won't learn anything about Free Music or the

Melanette machine or Grainger glides accomplished
by the PG System Kangaroo. *Lulu's* listed,
*Lute* and *Lur*, but not PG's *A Lot of Rot for Cello*.


5.

Anyhow, *Brigg Fair*. The brown wax cylinders revolved
to capture every bleat & twiddle of the lads from
Lincolnshire whose mix of Dorian Aeolian Ionian

scaled up and down the modes the way their fathers had
before the sons had left for towns and music hall.
He scored it with the jagged rhythms and the ornaments

intact. He scored it with the slides and hugged himself
with joy. He rose up in the morning with the lark
and beat himself until he bled. He broke all out in clover.

6.

And no one knew quite what *The Warriors* was.
Not Lady Elcho in her country house, the PM's mistress
and the friend of H.G. Wells; not all the Wedgwoods

or the Wedgwood-Benns; not John Singer Sargent
or his spiffy sitters or the Balfours in their motor car.
It didn't just sing *Willow Willow*, not just *Shepherd's Hey*.

Did it appeal or appall? The rich were not apprised.
While Stabat Mater nursed *le vice anglais*,
it wore out three conductors and an offstage band.


7.

If he could call himself a tone-wright & his music tonery,
he'd purge the spirochete that gnawed in Greek
and Latin at the mothertongue's profoundest roots.

He said he wasn't democratic but a-chance-for-all-y,
and he'd pound out all his tone-works
on keyed-hammer-strings. Blue-eyed English word-seeds

should replace all but the most un-do-with-outable
post-Hastings-French-begottens too. He'd oh stick-to-it-
ively drive himself to overset his thot-plan into deeds.


8.

Or go to Norway, visit Grieg. Introduce Duke Ellington
to Delius. He'd play the Green Man guising like
a geezer's dream of Morris-dancing tribes. He wore

a coat from which there dangled gewgaws & galoshes,
pencils, pens & manuscripts all tied on with
little bits of string: his only suitcase was a suite of songs.

His robin was to the greenwood gone, his Kammermusik
Strathspey in the hills. If he wasn't Grettir he'd be
Gershwin oh or Mowgli in a decorated plagal & in G.

9.

But how did one make sounds that were the sea?
In what key was a cloud? Did winds blow sharp or flat?
And when his lovers beat him with the whips

how was he to score his mother's lips?
Must he orchestrate an algolagnia for algophobes?
He'd grow all logarithmical

at loggerheads with Logos on the Loften Isles.
Blue-eyed English queried him—asked the why-grounds
for the hand-claps in the puzzle-wifty towns.

# Master Class

Well, then, one more time.

*Auf dem Flüsse* . . . where you
failed to emphasize the consonants enough
and your crescendo did not swell.
*Der du so lustig rauschtest* . . .
*Liegst kalt.* It's icy, understand?
What does a heartbeat sound like under ice?
Like this like this.
Let yourself be overcome by grief.

You can't? All right. Then let yourself
be overcome by joy.
Touch her and embrace her
as you did one summer on that river bank.
Unlace her bodice then. Your hand.
Right here. Heart, your heart
must break must break
because you know that she will die.

You are so young. You think these are clichés.
Your heart has never broken,
but it will. When I was young Isolde
Tristan died for me. I died for him.
You think this life is only song.
Begin again: Perhaps you favor French?
I am so old so old
and yet I do remember every touch.

So touch me. Here. Begin again, in French.
Shall you become my Pierrot Lunaire?
I'll sing for you from Berlioz:
*Ma belle amie est morte.*
You've never heard, I guess, of Gautier.
But if you care you'll die for me:
you'll die you'll die.
Here is the poison and the glass.

I am the mistress here, the maestro too.
This is my master class.
When you come, you'll sing it as I say.
You'll rhyme your *do*
with dildoe if I like.
You'll sing it sweetly while I play.
*Der du so lustig rauschtest* . . .
You'll sing it for me every day.

# Diminished Third

I. Expectation

The woman clad in white, large red roses
shedding petals from her dress, expects
the unexpected, wanders through a moonlit woods
where, God knows, anyone might stumble
on their lover's corpse . . .
                    Even Schoenberg
in Vienna in *Erwartung*, improvising
ostinatos, overriding bars, or Hohenzollern Isoldes
spiking Bismarck helmets at the stars—

Even Moses, who could only speak, exclaiming
*Ich will singen*,
counting on his finger tips the laws.


II. Doctor Faust

Boxed by Thomas Mann into a magic square
with megrims, paedophiles and fictive sounds,
A.S. rages over stolen property, the rape and insult
perpetrated by this syphilitic Leverkühn who writes

a serialism no one ever heard. And yet he'd said himself
that music was a word, that language was a kind
of music too: Had in fact some rowdy losal out of hell
so pricked his blood with sophistries that nosey

novelists could smell the sulphur in his permutations?
Did *Volk* and *Führer* grow dodecaphonic in his
retrogrades, inversions; Hetaera Esmaralda somehow

ciphered in the h-e-a-e flat of it? *Sator Arepo
tenet opera rotas*. The opera would circle, right enough.
And the sower would sue for his tenet. In tenebrae.

### III. The Golden Calf

*Aron, was hast du getan*

This Sprechstimme! This old dogmatic honky rapper
here before his time among the Angels.
He'd lecture all the Jews as all the Jews go down
all over Europe. He's safe and sound. His friend
is Mr. Gershwin and he beats the younger man
at tennis, ping pong, chess. He cannot win a Guggenheim,
cannot get performed.

Around him nothing but the idols
and the kitsch and the clichés. He's heard that in this
land of plenty no one gets a second act;
he cannot score a third and that's a fact.
Still the old Dodecaphon speaks while Aaron sings:
*Ich will singen dinga dinga ding!*
Anyone might stumble on a lover's corpse.

Is he Moses, Aaron, or their contradiction burning
in his brain like Leverkühn's disease?
*Darf das Leid, mein Mund, dieses Bild machen?*
Gershwin whistles happily: *I got plenty o' nuttin.*
Schoenberg spricht like eine glückliche hand:
*Das Grenzenlose! Boundlessness!*
Constellation upon constellation whirls.
Harmonielehre multiplies
by twelves through some 2000 bars and dies
with Volk and Führer.
So if the end, as Schnabel says, will justify the means,
you might as well have a nice day.
Why not keep on smiling while you
take the line of most resistance, even in LA?

# A Note on Barber's *Adagio*

    . . . Back in Autumn 1963
Samuel Barber was alone and driving through
November rain in Iowa or Kansas.
When he turned on his radio he heard
them playing his *Adagio for Strings*.
Sick to death of his most famous composition,
he turned the dial through the static
until once again, and clearly—
the *Adagio for Strings*. When a third station, too,
and then a fourth, were playing it, he thought
he must be going mad. He turned off the radio
and stopped the car and got out by a fence
staring at the endless open space in front of him
where someone on a tractor plowed
on slowly in the rain . . .

The president had been assassinated
earlier that day, but Barber didn't know it yet.
He only knew that every station in America was playing
his *Adagio for Strings*.
He only knew he didn't know
why he should be responsible for such an ecstasy of grief.

*For Dónal Gordon*

# Sadnesses: Black Seas

I

*Tristia, tristia*: Tomis or Constanța
Getae or Romanian might hear . . . might go and hide
heedless of a rhetoric resounding to its own

its onerous exemplum *adynata, adynata*: Naso
whose impossibilities would rage like Dido
hurling Latin in Aeneas' wake: O Divine Augustus

bitch of an apotheosis who recoiled, call, recall
those numbers moving with a grace that no one
south of Petersburg but Alexander Pushkin

could recite that song of bodies changing
into other bodies: Mandelstam prefiguring his own
departure into darkness gaudy indigence behind

beyond the poverty of happiness: eye of Eisenstein
plotting golden sections as caesurae thinking
two & three and two & three the empty baby carriage

bumping down Odessa steps the sly and hungry
host in naval whites at Yalta grinning at the crippled
president the portly flushed personified PM:


II

*Tristia, tristia: adynata, adynata:*
Scythians leap up from rocks look out from trees
as cameras grind in faithless documentary

and who can tell from just that word *departure*
how long spindles hum and shuttles flutter
back and forth to measure everything that's happened

happening again but this time without either
wax or bronze: *tristia, tristia:*
all the rivers flow back up to mountain streams

the horses of old Helios stumble in their course the sea's
aflame the plow of earth cleaves heaven:
General Insov was a loyal friend but what to do

with this new Governor Vorontsov good Ovidius
except go fuck his wife:
the field of honor is as boring as the gaming board:

*adynata, adynata:* Dr Smirnov will be shot close up
his pince-nez broken in his face if someone finds a man to play
the priest the sailors can be executed underneath a tarp

but what to do with all these little countries after such a scene
but swallow them: a ship might just as well
be named for Pushkin as Potemkin: Ovid has his statue now

and Stalin Churchill Roosevelt
it's true the birds are indiscriminate it's best no doubt
to be unknown a decent anonymity and

Mandelstam says women weave the men fall down in fields.

# Persistent Elegy

*(Shortly before the 1994 South African election my former student, Clare Stewart, was murdered in KwaZulu, probably by an Inkatha hit squad)*

And now at last Nelson Mandela's elected.
But what of my student, Clare?
Would she have danced as she had expected?
They don't even number the dead in Rwanda.
She raises her hand in the air.
What did she do in KwaZulu to anger Inkatha?

She sits in my class long ago taking notes.
This is my student, Clare.
Volunteers have busily counted the votes.
She wakes to the voices of children.
Her daughter's among them there.
What did she do in KwaZulu to anger Inkatha?

No volunteers can describe what nobody sees.
She leaves a note in the mission.
She walks by the lake, the flowering trees.
Observers say the election is fair.
She gets in a pick-up, drives from the village.
She raises her hand in the air.

She tries to answer the question.
What did you do in KwaZulu to anger Inkatha?
What is the answer, Clare?
They don't even number the dead in Rwanda.
Nobody's counting there.
But what did she do in KwaZulu to anger Inkatha?

She raises her hand in the air.
And now at last Nelson Mandela's elected.
What of my student, Clare?
She never arrives where she is expected.
Everyone's weeping there.
What did she do in KwaZulu to anger Inkatha?

What of my student, what of my student, Clare?

# My Mother's Webster

She'd never tell me how to spell a word;
*Go look it up*, she'd say. She'd say *It's there in Webster*,
pointing to the battered blue and dog-eared dictionary
that she'd lugged from Georgetown to Columbus long
before those Anglo-Saxon expletives she said offended her
entered the American Heritage. I find it at the bottom of a box
unpacking things I thought to save when she turned vague,

lost the words she'd loved, and started groping for a few
remembered monosyllables to get her through a day of
meals, treatments, therapies, and baths at Olentangy Home.
Her house is sold; she's 92; and I decide to look it up
when I'm unsure about how one spells *Houyhnhnm*
and want to write a footnote citing Swift in *Gulliver*.
The facing page is black with marginalia; it's in her hand.

What alchemy is this? *A curse on Sally Smothers*
she has written, circled, arrowed to *hostility*
in one direction, *hothead* in another. *Turn the page*
she writes, and there beside the underlined *horned toad*
and *hornet* she abbreviates, *S.S.*, with arrows to *horrendous*.
She writes: *My friends: Eleanor, Elizabeth, and Jean.*
She writes: *The boy I do not love: Jason Dean: ZZ.*

Some words are simply canceled: *housewife* with an X,
*hooker* with a line; the illustrations under *horseshoe*
toss her up to *horah*, ring her to *hosanna*; *horn of plenty* is
a *cornucopia*, and that is circled six or seven times.
Next to *horologe* she writes *ding-ding* and clearly likes
*hornswoggle*, prints in little caps: *They'll do it every time.*
She writes *I'll host a hostage in the hostel, my hors d'oeuvre!*

Who is this language sprite? It seems to be my mother
talking to herself in 1917. There's still heavy fighting on
the western front; her father has just died; she'll meet *my* father
in another seven years. There is no sulfa yet, no penicillin;
Eleanor and Jean will get the post-war flu and not survive.
I've never heard her mention Jason Dean. She will, in fact,
become a housewife and she'll outlive Sally Smothers

that old hothead she called *hornet* and *horned toad*.
The goddesses of seasons, Horae, might have taught her
in good time a ripe Horatian patience as she gazed
at *horoscope* and then *horizon*—looked up from the page
and out her bedroom window at the *horos*, boundary,
tangent plane across the surface of the globe defining
the conjunction of the earth and sky. She writes:

*I guess that means about as far as I can see.*
There's not a mark here or an indication that she saw her
future linked to *hospital* or *hospice*—
nor to *Houyhnhnms,* rational and gentle creatures
one might like for neighbors even at the Olentangy Home
and whose name I cannot spell. I can hear her say again
*Well go and look it up, It's there in Webster,*

meaning this particular blue book, and not some other.
I'd look her up herself if I could find her. She's always in,
but she is never there. She's here in 1917 and not hornswoggled
or intimidated or a hostage in some hostel where they
do it every time. There's a horseshoe on her door.
There's not a single cloud on the horizon and it's June.
She'll be her own hors d'oeuvre and dance the horah round

a horn of plenty. She writes: *I'm Thirteen in Three Days.*

# The Singing

Now we could talk. Too late,
too long ago I see you
in that chair and see
myself unwilling and impatient

and so full of hurry that I
hurt to get away and say
some quick and careless thing
which turns out to be all

I managed as the final words
I spoke to you. But now,
now we could talk. I have grown
patient. I sit as you once sat

alone most days and stare at nothing.
I know—too late, too well—what
you might say, or rather might have said,
what I will never now respond to you

but only mutter to myself or into darkness.
It sounds like sorrow. I mean the sound
of it is sorrow as some kind of song.
It's not so much a saying, then, as singing?

Did you want to sing to me that day
some twenty years ago, for me to sing to you?
Dear God what kind of song? What sorrow
sings what wretchedness to bed?

You did not go to bed. You sat. Your heart.
More rest from sitting up all night
than lying down. And all night long you sang.
Sang only to yourself because

there's no one ever who will listen
to such song. I know. I sing.
We'd sing that song together if you
were alive—the only one you sang,

the only one I sing beneath what talk
I can what tense I cannot manage
knowing far too late too well how long
you sat in what was never silence

what was never anything but song.
Now we could talk. Now we'd keep our silence
perfectly and hear each other sing.
Your past my future in that present when

impatient I heard nothing and went out.

# Left Hands and Wittgensteins
*For Roy Fisher at seventy and, inter alios, Leon Fleisher, Blaise Cendrars*

Paul's brother Ludwig the philosopher had said
*the world is everything that is the case*
in case you lost your arm. In case you could not play
for all the world. *No left hand*
we used to say as glib precocious critics of the young
Ahmad Jamal, one of us the southpaw pitcher
on the high school baseball team who struck out every
righthand batter in the junior league.
But Paul was *all* left hand who bitched at both Ravel
and Sergei Prokofiev but nonetheless
performed their music no right hand would ever play.
The world was everything that was the case
when Blaise Cendrars also lost his arm. In that same war.
In that same war where everything that was the case
exploded in the world. My friend the southpaw pitcher studied
in the end with Leon Fleisher who awoke one day
with no right hand as a result of carpal-tunnel stress. A syn-
drome: drone, his repertory was diminished but he played
Prokofiev he played Ravel, and all thanks due to Wittgenstein
whose world was everything that was the case.

Left hand, left wing? Roy, are all right-handers Tories
in their bones? They'd case your joint as if
they'd lost most everything left in the world.
(Or would you pack them in your case with all the world
except for B and exit in that key?) I weep
for your right arm, your stroked-out days of therapy,
your egging on your brain to find a few more millimeters
of its limb. But what's permission but commission
to a left-hand poet, left-hand pianist at seventy?
You might well go ask Wittgenstein, might well ask Cendrars.
Then go ahead—put the piano at risk, put the poem
in jeopardy: Millennium's a comin' after, Roy:
If anything could be the case
*the world is everything that is the case.*
Are those iambs, da-dah da-dah? Is that in 4/4 time?

# Reception

When the tired old poet's genuine modesty
and quiet life in the small university town
had finally made him all but invisible in the larger
world of literature, his former friend arrived

out of the past for a visit between readings
and appearances on television talk shows.
When the old poet's wife thought she heard
the condescension in the faint praise

the famous writer offered of what would be
her husband's final book, she took him aside
to fill up his wine glass and quietly said
*You know, Ernest's poems have always been*

*better than yours, which are full of
bombast and pretension.* Although I wasn't
meant to hear that, I did. Remembering it now,
I also think of Ernie telling me one night

about the way Eileen, young and pretty then
and not just some professor's wife,
used to dance like Carmen on the tables
of a local Polish bar . . .

# Unfinished

I. Haydn

　　. . . just those lines by Gleim,
*Der Greis* a part song now divided
among parts for voiceless strings that
whispered wordlessly *Hin ist alle meine
Kraft, alt und schwach bin ich* . . .
His strength . . . and all his skill . . .
Also printed on a card the servant gave
to those who'd come around & ask
for more. No more. No strength. No craft.
He'd hole-up like some crofter mumbling
*I am old and weak.* Two movements
in D minor of the last quartet just stop at
*Menuetto ma non troppo Presto.*
Then the four-part setting of the fifty
silent words that ended *Ein harmonischer
Gesang . . . mein Lebenslauf*


II. Schubert

The B Minor torso not unveiled, of course,
until December 1865. By then, all his friends
had also died. Two years earlier, sections
of his *Lazarus* cantata were performed. He had in fact
emerged quite often from his tomb, and while one
critic spoke in wonder of his "posthumous diligence"
another warned against "the adulation of
his relics." Endless bits and pieces and a range
in scale: a tenth symphony, the opera called
*Der Graf von Gleichen,* tossed-off riffs
of uncompleted *Lieder,* sketches for a symphony in D,
*Adrast* and *Sakuntala, Quartettsatz,*
a piano sonata in C, endless spare or
missing parts. You could construct with some

of these a Schubert of your own, and many
people tried. Was it protofascist Metternich Vienna
at his throat that made his doppelgänger
sing the *Agnus Dei* of the E-flat mass?
The Karlsbad Degrees and Count Sedlnitzky
drove his good friend Johann Senn
to exile and arrested his own work. His illness
did the rest. Charged with an "opprobrium of language,"
his optative became oracular in Heine, but his
doppelganger sang the *Agnus Dei* of the E-flat mass


III. Shostakovich

        ... and why not
give the opus number of that Gogol opera
left behind in Leningrad to Stalin's
NKVD choristers for song and dance,
*Otchizna* obbligati very much obliged?
For unacknowledged legislators, 63 might
suit the People's Commissariat to an ironic t.
A little joke on uncle Joe's police
from the abandoned *Gamblers*, scoundrel
fragments only sung out posthumously
three years after the sonata for viola
which had quoted them. Quoted them
in what became his actual farewell—omissions long
admitted in commissions from the state—
to Leningrad & Moscow & in fact not least
to Gogol's ghost still singing Gavryushka's song
about the better life in Ryazan and haunting
through a nearly empty Gulag

# The Lyric Suite: Aldeburgh Festival, Snape

Consummate in sound, *appassionato*,
Alban Berg's unconsummated love for Werfel's sister!
Her initials, H and F, conjoined with his own
as in a page illuminated in the mind
from *Kells* or Lindisfarne, locked to Schoenberg's mathematics.
Hanna's copy of the score alone
sang the unsung text, penciled in and set
but then erased. The quote from *Tristan*.
Then the *De Profundis Clamavi* of Baudelaire.

How alien this passion sounds arching out of Hanna's Prague
of 1925 and into evening mists of a tranquil Suffolk summer,
weaving through the reeds around the Alde
and reaching on towards Orford church to dissipate
like unfulfilled desire.
And yet how I desire you, listening and failing
to listen to this sound, drifting
on a music of my own, then returned abruptly to this hall
by stricture and precision.

*Allegretto gioviale* . . . and the theme,
the twelve-tone row, enclosed by her initials.
"No hint," he wrote, "of tragedy to come."
Near us here, the old mill at Letheringham
is still. The wheel turned the year they wrote
the Doomsday Book. I've known this landscape
now for twenty years, felt it utterly
suffused with the presence of the woman here
beside me. Heavy rain this morning
sent the peahens scurrying, a huddle of ducks
and guinea fowl disappearing among reeds.
Daffodils were thick along the stream.
A tree trunk full of moss. Small brick cottage,
dull red tiles on its roof. . . . I sit
beside the woman I have loved for twenty years.
I think of someone else.

I think of you, and I desire you, listening
and failing to listen to this sound,
as he desired you himself, straining for the boundary
of expression as the spindle of his time unwound,
listening and failing to listen
to the voices of Vienna, generations of them
singing in a thousand violins, all those
strings attached to every note he wrote, every string
played pizzicato saying *du du du*
and meaning *her*, and yet he too desired you,
wrote his program into what I hear
and do not hear, writing letters with his other hand
to say *I was unfaithful to you only during
a performance of the Mahler, only
because Mahler took my mind from you, my love,
but only for an hour,* thinking really *Hanna, Hanna,*
whom he called Mopinka, and his program,
*amoroso,* then *misterioso* and *ecstatico.* . . .

And why should not your name be Hanna? since
I cannot name you? since you have today no other name?
since I think of you as *thou* but need to call
out now, to call out and to whisper both, to call
you by some name, to whisper in the silence between
movements *Do you hear the singing now?* to be assured
that no one does, and not to mean do you,
do *you* hear it who are part of it as word and sound,
nor in any way confuse you with my love,
my love, linking your initials in some page
illuminated in the mind from *Kells* or Lindisfarne—
Hanna, then, Mopinka.

*Do you hear the singing now?* But now there is no singing,
was no singing but for those who heard it
in imagination, two of them and two of us . . .
She shakes her head, and in the space between

the *presto delirando* and the *largo*
landscape opens from the hall beside the Alde
and into time. A secret name, and an acknowledged name,
inhabit it. And are there always two?
The mill stream at Letheringham flows beneath
the wheel, the Alde by Snape and Iken,
then below the Orford castle keep and to the sea.
Water fowl leave their hieroglyphic prints
on mud as slick as oil while the tidal river shrinks
into a ribbon and the boats lie crazily
at angles in the ooze and weeds. Darkness comes
to Tunstall Forest, Campsea Ash and Woodbridge.
Again the quartet plays, *desolato* now.

*My cry arises from a landscape with no brook
or tree, no field or flock, where air is lead and where
in shadows terror looms* . . . As if some tenor
might emerge from such a place and stretch his voice
four octaves on the rack of *Fleurs du Mal* . . .
*The cold terror of this icy star . . . and of this
night . . . So slowly does
the spindle of our time unwind* . . . When all is done
we do what is expected, clap our hands
and shuffle up the isle while four musicians,
after bows, pack up instruments and leave the quiet hall.
Berg's Helene listened to this suite one summer night
some sixty years ago. Who knows what she heard?
She spoke of neither fear nor of desire.
When all was done, she did what was expected,
clapped her hands and shuffled
up the aisle while the four musicians,
after bows, packed up instruments and left the quiet hall,
*so slowly did the spindle of their time unwind.*

And now the landscapes cease
to alternate, to overlap: Prague returns to Prague,

Vienna to Vienna, and I am here in Suffolk by the Alde.
I walk away in moonlight like some dizzy Pierrot,
some Pierrot Lunaire . . .
Beside me there is just one woman,
steady and serene—
and silent as the silent endless last indifferent sky.

# Black Dog

The black dog's in the room with us
and yet we joke about his bark.
He's bitten Joe. He's bitten me.
At the moment, he's asleep. We'd rather
have a large indifferent cat beside the hearth,
but somehow this black dog came in again
who's all too keen to get involved.
He ate the dinner that we couldn't eat ourselves.
He picked his teeth with our pencils.
We'd like to write him off, but he's
written *Canine* on our poems. He doesn't
get our jokes and we can't just get up
and go. We'd talk about our travels
but this isn't Argos sleeping here.
We're left with what he'll let us do,
which isn't much: We'll only speak of him
until he hears the wolf-calls in the night &
wakes up from his dream of our confinement.

*for Joe Francis Doerr*

# Ohio Forebears

### Albert C.

He'd vaccinate at gun point if he had to
when there was an epidemic. Out he'd go
in what his son still called a "buggy"
in the 1940s. Friendly with the gun strapped

on his hip, he'd had it since a rebel
shot him through the elbow in the Civil War.
Eventually, he lost the arm, but not
before he used both hands delivering

uncounted babies in Gilboa and McComb.
Born on the battle's anniversary, his son
was given "Shiloh" as a middle name.
With 10,000 dead on either side, who would

light the candles on his cake? Beauregard retreated.
Pittsburgh Landing held. But the dark
in the covenant was truly arked.
Albert kept his arm in a bottle of formaldehyde

underneath a cupboard by the coal chute.
Now and then he'd go and have
a look at it. The gun was given in his will
to Edward Shiloh and the arm

was buried with him when he died.

## Edward Shiloh

The gun was quite antique in '98, but
he took it with him anyway. No Rough Rider,
he nonetheless claimed Teddy R as his
own man and spoke with jingo confidence.

Although he never got to Cuba, Supreme Court
pages said they'd seen him in his uniform
that hangs in tatters in my closet by
the judge's robe that he and then my father wore.

He was distinguished for the wisdom and the style
of his opinions which are studied even now
in schools of law. He'd pace the upstairs study floor
incanting: *Goddamn the goddamn damn.*

My father said to him one night: *I wish you'd taught
me how to curse.* His bookshelves bulged
not only with The Law, but poetry:
With Kipling & with Whitman & with Tennyson . . .

At ten I sat there on his floor with Gunga Din.
I loved each button on his uniform, his
epaulettes, the dull dress sword. But most of all
the pistol brought from Shiloh with a shattered arm.

A large bronze bust they made of him
and put it in the State House where for fifty years
he was Ohio's Justice Holmes. The plaster cast,
intact for many months, shattered into pieces

in the hallway where it stood beside our phone.
A call from someone with bad news—
all about the trouble I'd got into at my school—
and suddenly the patriarch was dust.

The papers said he'd slipped and fallen
from a window where he tried to show exterminators
where the squirrels got into the house. But I knew
this synchronicity was all my fault. Although the bronze

statue stood upon its pedestal, I knew
that phone call somehow broke the plaster cast and
pitched him out the window, too. I believed in the uncanny:
Pittsburgh Landing calling yet to Shiloh & to Beauregard,

the finger on a severed arm pointing straight at me.


### John Marshall

It's hard to be a judge and named for Marshall
but at least he wasn't monikered
for some battle in the Spanish War. The family
used to sing the bully anthems and they all

remembered the Maine. He missed the war his
own generation fought because rheumatic fever
licked his heart with flame and made him, unlike
Albert C and Edward S, unfit to serve.

His ill health followed him in ways I never knew
until he died. What he wanted was to serve.
The state. His family. Something, anyway.
When Edward Shiloh fell out of that window

and I thought my truancies from school had been
the cause, he won the unexpired term
and wore his father's robe as if it were a uniform.
And that was what destroyed him.

He was a shy and rather simple man and what
he could do well he did before
he had to live up to his name. His level
was Municipal, and traffic court his calling.

Although they made no bust of him, they cast
his name in bronze and screwed it
to his office door. It might as well have said:
*Give up hope all Ye who enter here.*

He entered every day. A hundred yards away
his father's statue stood.
He stuck it out for something like a dozen years
and then resigned, humiliated by his frailty.

### John Edward

Ohio forebears on a shelf imported from
all over: Pooh and Rupert,
Paddington and Roosevelt, Delmore Schwartz.
And books to tell their tales.

Even Pooh's is sad, abandoned in the end
by the boy he loved and served.
To all of them, I'm Albert's severed arm,
I'm Edward Shiloh's plaster cast,

John Marshall's dickey heart, the clumsy foot
of Paddington at tea time—
a badly broken covenant with all
of them and exiled in a place

I thought I chose that isn't Rome or Tomis
either one but closes borders on your
marches where the cars are stalled and all
the horses sleeping in their harnesses

& Sherman's not recruiting any more, Ohio.

# Variations on the *Song of Songs*
*For Laura and Elliot*

What shall a father say to his daughter, the bride?
The beams of our house were of cedar.
The rafters were branches of fir.

And then to the bridegroom, what can he say?
This woman you love once was a laughing child.
The beams of her house were of cedar.

And as she grew up she also grew down—
Down into the center of things,
and up where the beams were of cedar—

and there in her house she grew wise, though at first
nobody noticed, for she was a laughing child
and her rafters were branches of fir.

But the cedar and fir came from a song,
the rafters and beams were all singing:
And out of the song came a bridegroom who said:

What shall a man say to this woman, his bride?
May the beams of our house be of cedar,
our rafters the branches of fir,

May we sing out *Shir ha-Sharim*
For this daughter and son, this woman and man:
May we celebrate with this song:

Rafter and beam, Song of all Songs, *Shir ha-Sharim*.

# Letter to an Unborn Grandson
*For Ian Joshua, Laura & Elliot*

Ian Joshua!—for that will be your name—
    I've written many poems
        as elegies to people who have died,

but haven't yet addressed one
    to a person not quite with us yet.
        I'm so slow at writing poems these days

you may well have been born
    before I'm finished,
        but my intention is to have this

in your mother's hands at least a week before
    your scheduled birth.
        I need to tell you this and that about

its form and why I've chosen it.
    William Carlos Williams, a doctor
        who was also one of our best poets,

thought the three line stanzas
    that he started writing late in life
        had finally captured the American idiom

he'd sought in all his writing
    in what he came to call a "variable foot."
        I've studied it a bit and have to tell you

that in fact I can't quite figure out
    what he meant
        & don't know if he really knew himself

in any kind of analytic way.
    But it doesn't really matter since the fact remains
        that he wrote these poems

that move a little bit
    like this
        in stepped down three-ply lines

late in life and deep in illness
    which have moved me off and on
        for many years. I've always loved

the great poems of the old—by men like
    Yeats and Hardy,
        men like my old friend Sandeen,

a poet whom your mother knew
    when she was young
        and used to visit mainly for the excellent

desserts his wife prepared—Eileen,
    in Ernie's life a counterpart of Williams'
        Floss, to whom he

wrote the best of all his later poems, whose love & care
    kept him going once his
        health began to fail. Now that I am

growing old myself, I read these poets even
    more, seeking to discover
        what the next thing is that life has got in store

for me. It's oddly not unlike when I was adolescent
    and read erotic work
        to learn about the mysteries of sex that

I anticipated with such eagerness. We didn't have
    explicit movies then or porn-
        ographic magazines, but D.H. Lawrence,

Henry Miller, and Anaïs Nin did fine.
    The old poets
        also wrote erotic poems when they

were young, and that's perhaps the reason
    they could write so well
        about the dark and final death that

followed all the little deaths from
    which one got right
        up & out of bed & put one's pants

back on, and went about one's
    daily work. It may seem odd to write to you
        at your age about sex,

but, Ian Joshua, that's the reason
    you got where you are
        right now. Because of that and love.

And there's another reason
    that I'm writing to you in this form.
        When your mother

started getting quite impatient to be born
    we went off quickly
        to the local hospital. It wasn't far, just

two blocks away. I grabbed a book
    to take along which
        happened to be William Carlos Williams'

all but posthumous last book.
    In those days older male obstetricians
        still liked fathers

out of sight for a delivery,
    and so I sat with other nervous men, reading
        Williams, waiting for your mother

to be born. I had reached page sixty-three,
    'The Turtle,' when
        a nurse came in and asked me if I'd

like to see my daughter.
    And there your mother was—
        looking wide-eyed at the world

and making a terrific row. I stared at her amazed
    and wrote down in the margin
        of the Williams book *Laura born*,

*October 23 at 9:04 p.m., right in the*
    *middle of this poem.*
        There's more. 'The Turtle' has a dedication:

*For My Grandson.* He'd commissioned, evidently,
    from his grandfather a poem
        about a turtle, the grandson's only pet,

and Williams wrote it happily. *Upon his back,*
    he said, *shall ride*
        *to his conquests, my Lord, you!*

*He is all wise*
    *and can outrun the hare.*
        Williams by that time could hardly

walk, could barely type, sometimes
    couldn't even speak
        so that family & his friends & all

 the many poets who admired him
   could understand what he meant.
     But he went on writing poems,

sometimes feeling guilty for
   the time he'd spent among the avant-gardists
     of New York

when he should have been with patients
   back in Rutherford.
     I can easily imagine now his gentle hands

upon your mother's belly,
   his stethoscope listening to your heartbeat.
     He had delivered hundreds and

hundreds of babies in his day,
   one of them the Rutherford policeman
     who led off the procession

to the cemetery where they buried him.
   Stroke after stroke
     he grew more feeble, poem after poem

he thought might be his last. 'The Turtle'
   came quite late.
     Ian Joshua! It's hard to be a poet; don't

go down that path
   unless you've got a lifeline
     to the practicalities of living like

this doctor did; it's a risky business
   and it makes you an observer
     even of your own observations.

It makes you peek and pry;
    even he invaded privacies
        like I'm invading yours right now

before you're even born!
    Some free advice: Love your mother
        who will love you very much even

when you don't believe she does.
    Love your father equally.
        And when you grow as they say "up"

find some good that you can do
    with work however difficult
        that brings you joy & brings nobody harm.

When Williams praised the calling of the poet
    —and he often did—
        and said "I am a poet, I am!"

and when he praised Imagination and its forms,
    I think he must have known
        that it was all those souls that he had

helped into the world, bright new lives
    like yours about to start
        that in the end redeemed both him and everything

he wrote. And so to each a turtle:
    To you, your mother, and your dad. From me,
        this scribbling in the margin of a doctor's book.

III

# Swell
*For Diana*

### I

The lake was swell that year. The fishing too
was swell both there and in the rivers, but especially swell
was that one lovely girl among the group from
Horton Bay. It was 1920 and he'd lived
somehow through shelling at Fossalta di Piave that
he'd write about, and then escaped the influenza
which had killed more people than the war itself,
among them Edward, eldest son of my own
Grandfather M, himself a veteran of the Spanish War
and Spanish flu . . .
                    In 1950 there I am
with my one fish, a bass. I caught it trolling from a boat
in Walloon Lake and someone took my picture
holding it up high. That's the full extent of my experience
and success as angler. But it was swell that day.
I was ten and I'd been on the lake since dawn.
They all say things are swell in early Hemingway.
We say things are great, even when they're not, even
when they're only fair-to-middling, even when
they're only average to a fault. Great time. Great lake.
Great girl. Those things that were swell.
We say it sometimes with a lean sarcastic sneer
and sometimes really mean it.

Two or three years later I began to read him.
I thought he was just great. Who didn't in those days
before they wrote his life, counted up his whiskies and his pills,
and told his secrets as he went to seed somewhere out in Idaho
and at the Mayo Clinic where they gave him so much
ECT he thought his house in Cuba was in Kenya
and his second wife his first, his third some kind of matador.
I read about Nick Adams on the lake and all those
summer people first at Horton Bay and then in Paris and
Pamplona. They all said swell and I thought they were great
and even read the prose aloud. The names of places

that I knew myself would make me dizzy with the recognition
as I whisperingly incanted them in bed where I was often ill:
*Petoskey, Charlevoix, Boyne Falls* . . .

        If I knew these I might know Paris too
and even some swell girl who'd maybe show me her swell cunt,
a word that Scribners didn't let him print but that I knew anyway
from dirty-talking Nell on Hudson Street. We'd summer up in
Michigan on Walloon Lake like he did. At Shadow Trails Inn. I loved
my father then the way he had loved his, who taught
him how to fish and hunt before he lost his mind
and put a bullet in his brain. I think my father took the picture.
There I am holding up my bass.


II

It's now 2000 and we can't find Windermere. Thirty years
between his final summer here and 1950; fifty years
between my one big catch and this boat on the lake without a line.
Things have not been swell, have not been great.
Well, sometimes they were swell: a while ago, & in another country.
His phrases stuck forever in your mind provided that
you read him very young.

        But this week is okay. We've taken walks,
eaten whitefish both at Pippin's and the Walloon Inn,
and tried to figure what it means at sixty still to be alive.
Who at ten or twenty sees himself in forty, fifty years?
Robert Lowell barely made it; Berryman,
who sat cross-legged in my Salt Lake City room
and recited every word verbatim of *A Clean, Well-Lighted Place*
only got to fifty-eight. He said that story was a poem, and
he was right. I'm older than my teacher was
when he died. I'm older than Lowell. About the age
when Hemingway, who, like his father, like crazy Mr. B,
knew he'd had enough.

          I haven't had enough.
I'm greedy and want more. I like it here on this swell lake
and looking at the shoreline passing by like print
you scan searching for that great passage you can't find
but once had known by heart. The one that either
let you through into some other world or knocked you dead.

To read at all when I first read meant simply to read him.
Misogynist or drunk, vain & boastful & commercially
successful ruin like they say, he gave me passage anyway
to pass on by, forgetting & ungrateful. Now I have no interest
in those other houses on the shore, even in what's left of
Shadow Trails Inn, which all at once I locate from a bright
configuration of some oddly angling birches
that I haven't seen for fifty years. When we were here before
I didn't know about his cottage. Windermere.
He couldn't find it either until Paris when he'd lost it
in his life to win it for his art.
And then began to say that certain things were swell:
a lake, a girl, a morning catch of trout.
A clean well-lighted place was only clean and bright.

There's yet another photograph of everyone
at Shadow Trails Inn. Everyone but me, so this time
I was the photographer. Not a single person there was left alive.
Dick and Mary, John and Lois, Jim and Florence,
Cousin Nancy, Uncle Bob—there they were against a wall,
the flag up flapping on the pole. Some firing squad
from *In Our Time* must have come and shot them where they stood,
and there was nothing I or anyone could do.
It must have happened as I turned and looked away.

III

        Just how old
was Nico A. when he walked all dazed & drawn through Italy,
when he finally laid that girl in Horton Bay
having slain the others anyway with rugged looks and laughter.
(Lots of irresistible bad rhymes with Hemingway.)
My wife was Adams too (Diana) when we met in 1966.
She was swell & great & it was London & in May.

She points at something from the bow. A scene straight
out of *Gatsby* in a stately choreography
on someone's lawn. The swells are dressed in morning suits,
although it's afternoon, and pastel-colored gowns, tinkling ice cubes
in their glasses waiting for the host and hostess
circulating on the terrace, pitchers in both hands, to pour another Pimms.
The rich are different from the rest of us, said Scott.
They have bigger boats. Ours is maybe fifteen feet, plus outboard.
In a larger craft than this, I did in fact reach Paris.
Reached Pamplona, too. It's taken me a lifetime to prefer it here.
When I met Diana at some crazy Sixties party
she was standing at the far end of a narrow room and
looking like an advert for the mini-skirt. Was she
the cover-girl of that month's issue of *Time Out*
that featured "The Most Stunning Birds in London"?
(Birds of course were women who were swell.)
Men would stop & stare at her in the street. One man
wrecked his car, craning for a better look.
I couldn't believe my luck. And now she points again:
at naked swimmers in the lake, breast and buttock visible
with each new stroke, heading
from that Daisy of a dock across the lake to Eagle Point.

I like the old man's late erotic work. The things he couldn't
publish and kept working on in spite of hopeless odds
against completing them. Scribners held *The Garden of Eden*
for decades. How he loved the way those three, those

two birds and the guy, try things out he now could never do.
And even Nick and Littless seem intent on incest as they
light out for the territory half a mile from here while Mr. Packard
at the shop detains the wardens blathering about tobacco.
Left unfinished, Nick's last story stops at *Sure* when Littless
asks *And will you read it? Or is it too old to read out loud?*
Too old to read out loud? She's brought along *Wuthering Heights*.
Or did she mean Am *I* too old to ask you for this gift?
He'll read to her. It's swell, and so is she. She cuts her hair
like Catherine on the Côte d'Azur, calls herself a boy.
She says that they'll have children, swings her child's legs
astraddle on his hips. Sure, he says, I'll read.

He stops it there. His friend E.P. got back to Italy because
the rich old novelist could write him a swell check.
E.P.: who said to Lowell he'd started with a swollen head
to end with swollen feet. Hem, who measured Scott's
small cock & told him, Look: it only counts engorged with blood.


IV

The bodies of the dead lay all around him, drained
of blood, all engorged with gangrenous corruption. He thought
he'd lose his leg, and by the time he knew he wouldn't
was in love. The story is well known.
The facts as he reported them from time to time are questioned,
but the story is well known. It was Red Cross for sure
and not Italian infantry in which he served, but what the hell.
Some of what he said he did he didn't really do.
But he was born to tell a tale or two. They dug the shrapnel
from his leg and tore apart his knee to reassemble it.
He thought one night he felt his soul ascend out of his body
and return. His lady married, in the end, somebody else;
He came back here to heal . . .
                                      We stopped in Horton Bay
to buy a paper at the general store. It seems to be

unchanged. The BBC had once brought in a film crew for a shoot
and asked the puzzled clerk: *Can we buy these?*
Presenting him a shopping list preserved for eighty years
scribbled out by Mrs. H, the doctor's wife.
They still sold everything except some kind of ghastly Spam.
Embarrassed that we only had a paper, I also
bought a bottle of Chablis. We've got it with us in the boat.
Was that the store where Mr. Packard had detained the wardens
letting Nick and Littless make their run?

The man next door at Red Fox Inn would know. He'll sell you
books or cook your lunch or put you up at night.
He's got the place declared a National Historic Site, and tells you
this is "Fox's House" in "Up in Michigan." Tempted
by a copy of *3 Stories & 10 Poems* which I had never seen, I
noticed it was Xeroxed in between the warping boards
he'd stitched and glued himself. He knew the canon like a Priest
his Bible, but he hadn't read or didn't like much else . . .
Mr. Faulkner? No. Mr. Fitz? A friend of Hem's. Mr. Joyce?
You mean that irksome Irishman? He'd made some maps with
marks and annotations noting where each incident occurred in all
the stories and he gave us free gummed labels saying
*Purchased from the heir of Volie Fox, fishing guru who taught
Hemingway his tricks.* We stuck one on the bottle of Chablis.

He had my number, though, and shouted out *Goodbye Professor!*
and I turned about to say, *well actually I don't teach Him,*
but only waved, and thought of one old Brother in the Art, fired both
by and for his genius at my place of work, teaching even
*Across the River* to his Freshmen, saying of poor Cantwell,
*If he could well he would well but he can't well.*
The students, still too young to get it, laughed politely, none
of them as yet with serious wounds.
My friend was early wounded though he'd not been in a war.
He too left his shit and fluids in a hole he'd
dug in lethal earth which had not blessed him for his works.

V

Well, the perks of academia. That's why you are here
says my antagonist, some voice internalized
of Mr. Volie Fox. It's called a leave. It's a sabbatical.
Get off my gown. I'll gouge your eye out
with the corner of my mortarboard.
You're corrupt as all the rest, says Volie Fox,
even though you don't talk theory and you evidently
like to read. But you can't fish.
What you really go for is what Packard at his general store
tells his wife he hates: Chautauquas. You like culture.
You'd rather go to them than to revivals where
at least they get worked up and fuck each other afterwards.
Packard liked young Nick because he saw him swelling up
with original sin. This fishing boat's a kind of
water-slumming and you can't spend half an hour
on the lake without a book & wine . . .

And yet the water sometimes blesses even lubbers
and their books. The swells of southern seas, rivers, lakes, fjords
and even damned up creeks like one I played in near my house
on Old Glen Echo Drive. All water's amniotic, nowhere Lethe,
and we watch with joy those naked girls swimming
there some fifty yards in front of us like two fine porpoises before
a ship that's making for a landfall. On land you do fall down,
so any fool builds his house or city near the ocean,
or the river or the lake. Even bourgeois mother's sons from
Oak Park Illinois were close enough to smell
Lake Michigan in western winds and bend to its bravado.
Colonel Cantwell sans Viagra lay beside his girl
in Venice; in that gondola he knew she was the angel of death,
but rocked with her on the canal. And at the start
young Nick, whose lover called him Wemedge, heard
along with waves that lapped on shingle there at Horton Bay,
*I love it, Wemedge. Love it. Wemedge, come.*

Chautauquas came with Methodists & Women's Christian Temperance
to Petosky, where also Sherwood Anderson had lost his
scalp, burlesqued in *Torrents of Spring*. Packard who dislikes
Chautauquas also rails against "resorters," "change-of-lifers"
sitting on hotel front porches in their rocking chairs.
He must have been a friend of Volie Fox.
His wife on culture: "Packard, I won't bother you with this,
but it really makes me feel swell."
And on her change-of-life: "I'm still all the woman you can handle,
aren't I now" . . .
                    We cut the outboard at the sand bar
and we open the Chablis. Still no sign of Windermere
that we can see. Diana points again. Unembarrassed, tall and brazen,
both the naked girls walk up on the sandy beach
and shake the water off their golden bodies like two dogs.
Then they turn to us and smile.


## VI

He turns to her and smiles. Sure, he says,
he'll read. He'd meant before, I now remember, that the books
she'd brought were all too old for her, but he's
agreed to read one anyway, "out loud." That way, he
explains, it lasts a longer time. So when she asks
"Is it too old?" she means of course "for someone of my age."
But he's persuaded by this point and opens Brontë,
does the whole Chautauqua for the sister-boy on his knee.
In Salt Lake City J.B. said: Matthias, don't
read Proust until you're over forty—and so of course I started it
at once, looking, as we do, for secrets someone
thinks we shouldn't yet be privy to.

So there it ends in the selva oscura with *Wuthering Heights*,
the wardens having left the store & on their trail.
Which means he couldn't finish it, or was it really done?
Nights when I'm afraid and cannot sleep, Diana often says

Then shall I read? She means of course "out loud."
She knows that way it lasts a longer time. I always ask
for something that's too young for me, more likely
*Pathfinder* than Proust. It's what we have invented to
shut down my fear, send me off onto some quiet lake of peace.
She'll say, Some boy's adventure maybe?
How about your macho friend E.H.?
And I'll say, Adams, that's not fair! But I end up with
what I liked the best when I was twelve, & that was Adams
fishing here in Michigan. We don't do Heathcliff at Chautauqua;
we just troll on out for my one bass.

Although right now, awake, the outboard dead,
we do not have a line or pole or net.
You don't get bass or trout or marlin with your mind alone
(even if it conjures tigers in your bed).
We sit here rocking in the shallows, drinking wine.
The naked girls are gone. Shadows fall across
the party on the lawn. I am content.
But that's what Faust says when he's done for,
when he gazes on his works of reclamation in the hands of
that Chautauqua in apotheosis, old Herr G.
So things can be too Swell for our own good, swell
out of hand, grow cosmic in their folding
space right over into time. It's just the wine, my love,
the rocking on these waves, and it will pass.
This started out to be a poem about a bass I caught when
I was ten. And never once again.
You'll read to me tonight, I know. Whether Proust or
Mother Goose, it does its work. It's no big show
at the Chautauqua with a smell of gaslight, but it's exactly swell
enough, no more. It's great. In my life it's starting to get late.
We haven't yet found Windermere
and now the sun has set entirely on the lake.

# Part Two

## *from* Kedging

### I

### Post-Anecdotal

> ...cannot you stay until I eat my porridge?
> —Will Kempe

# Post-Anecdotal

I

And then what? Then I thought of
What I first remembered:
Underneath some porch with Gide.
Oh, not with Gide. But after years & years
I read that he remembered what he first
Remembered, and it was that.

II

Not this: Someone calling me,
Johnny, Johnny. I was angry, hid.
It was humid, summer, evening.
I hid there sweating in the bushes
As the dark came down. I could
Smell the DDT they'd sprayed
That afternoon—it hung there in
The air. But so did the mosquitoes
That it hadn't killed. Johnny!
Oh, I'd not go back at all. I'd
Slammed the door on everyone.

# Kedging

                        's all you're good for
someone said. Is what? Your good

and for it. Not to fear: O all your
goods so far. Your good 4.

Your goods 5 and 6. With a little tug
at warp. So by a hawser winde

your head about. Thirty nine
among the sands your steps or

riddle there. Who may have
sailed the Alde is old now, olde

and addled, angling still for some
good luck. So labor, lad: *when other*

*moiety of men, tugging hard at kedge
and hawser, drew us from*

*the sand?* Brisk and lively in the
dialect East Anglian. *Ain't so well*

*as I was yesterday, for I was then
quite kedge. Even though I pull and*

*pole and persevere I'm blown to
windward. Winding still. Warping so*

*as not to weep, cadging as I can.*

# Hoosier Horologe

I

ON THE EARLY MANNER OF T.E. HULME

who had no later manner. But also
Hadn't pork chops in his poems!
Pink pigs for Impressionists, but
No ardoise / framboise for Mr. Whom.
Hulme, sir. And no E.P. in that T.E.
Matter, manner. Natter natter.
Only a Brit at the lip
Of a trench, smoking a Bosphorus gasper.
Only a moon torching a cloud.


II

ON THE LATER MANNER OF GEOFFREY HILL

You wonder where | that line I wrote has gone?
Famous in its time was "Where the tight ocean
Heaves its load." Some drunken sailor stumbling
From a pub and barfing in the street, I thought.
But cut for good as sóme kínd of penance.
Spondee, that. Berryman is somewhere in this mix.
And not just Manley Hópkins. Not just Milton either.
The sailor's name was Ocean, Legion, Seaman,
I forget. What load did he heave then, M & M?
The bloody weight of the whole | world!

# Corvo, Pessoa, di Camillo, etc.

Kevin Thomas Patrick Medina y Carrizo di Camillo,
That's your name. Your names. We all need
Three or four; we all should be Pessoa, Baron Corvo,
If we could be. But they, like you, were Catholic & I fear
This naming's pagan. Polytheists worship
Different gods in different names. Álvaro de Campos
Wouldn't write Ricardo Reis' poems. Just ask
Fernando. I'd never call you Tom or Pat. Nor would
One address the Baron—Frederick William Serafino
Austin Lewis Mary Rolfe—as Lew or Bill. Those names
Just seem dormant, somehow yet to come. I'm sorry
That we have to talk so much about the meds we take, the
Drugs intended by the medics to dispatch a name or two.
Rolfe was clearly paranoid, Pessoa was perhaps a
Schizophrenic. A critic of my own stuff wrote the other
Day that "although every poet must love names, JM
Loves them to excess." Kevin, I would name you
Pope if I were able, Hadrian the Eighth. I'd puff white
Smoke out of my ears and nose. Who else sends me,
Lapsed Presbyterian that I am, Happy Feast Day messages
(St. Matthias, 14 May), or, for years, prays for my lost
And disaffected daughter who could be in Indianapolis
Or, for all I know, in Venice like the Baron as a gondolier:
Her name the most beautiful of all. Anyway, I hope
That all the gods protect the powers and persuasions of
The names of the house of di Camillo. And that they feast
As one and several in the name of what they love.

# Polystylistics

Simeon had style, but only did
One thing—admittedly impressive, if unvaried.
Juggler, too, had just a single act,
And tossed his balls *before the Lord*.

Serial and several, boys! When
Menelaus asks for Proteus, he
Knows the servant of Poseidon turns
More tricks than Helen, and is

Hard to hold. Plainsong stylized the
Prayers: Singing at the monkish
Hours of Prime, Sext, Nones, no one's
Goods are godly. Seals only barked

One note to lost Achaeans. Steel as in
Stalin piercéd Shostakovich
But not Schnittke: Viz, his lecture at
The Moscow Music Congress, 1971.

Even *In Memoriam* can waltz on broken
Legs back from Leningrad to
Old Vienna, even a quartet can play its
Ending first and leap from Renaissance

Orlando Lassus to the *Grosse Fuge*. Hail,
Prince! If you hold Simeon, he only fears
A fall; Proteus may sing a pillar made of
Fire or water, but he sings. Stand to harms!

Poseidon at Apocalypse opens seven styles.

# Not Will Kempe

> *Only . . . that's no jest.*
> RALEGH

A fool brings the queen an asp;
Another leaves the king
When he's most needed—right
In the middle of the play.

I think a fool is in the doorway
Of my life, neither bringing
Anything just yet nor going off;
He's there, though, and watching.

It's so quiet I can hear him breathe.
We're not on stage, but I know
That I'm upstaged—and
It's so quiet I can hear him breathe.

# Christopher Isherwood Stands on His Head

Half way to a double dactyl with that title.
I think he stood like that for ten or fifteen minutes,
Which is almost worthy of hexameters.
Why was he standing on his head?
(I was standing on my feet, and mightily
Perplexed—a student down from Stanford
In L.A., looking at another kind of life.)
He said he'd finished his new novel
Just that day and thought he ought to celebrate.
And then stood on his head. He told me
That he'd picnicked recently with
Aldous Huxley—meant to be there at
The party—and the aging Chaplin, when they
Found themselves on someone's private property
Accosted by police. They were told they'd have
To leave. Huxley said: Do just let us finish lunch;
This is Charlie Chaplin, back for a visit to America.
The cop damn well knew Chaplin when he saw him—
Little guy with a derby, cane & funny walk—
These three trespassers could
Pack it up and move it out, he said—and that
Included Charlie Chan . . .
                            And I thought
I knew Aldous Huxley when I saw him—
Approached a tall man in a corner sipping wine
Who said—*But I'm Jeff Chandler, actually*!
Astonished, I stared at Chief Cochise, noble Indian
Hero of my childhood, Jimmy Stewart's friend,
Star of *Broken Arrow* which I'd seen a dozen times.
I could feel myself perspiring, and I
Couldn't think of anything to say. *Aldous Huxley is quite
Old*, he sniffed. *So is Charlie Chaplin, who is over there.
He's talking with Marlene Dietrich*, Chandler said—
Isherwood still standing on his head.

# Smultronstället

... and someone saying, *Yes*
*but Göran doesn't really speak good Swedish.*
I looked up, perplexed.
*Skanian*, he declared. *He's from the south*,
as all of us—Doctor Isak Borg and Marianne,
Sarah, Anders, and Viktor;
Susan, John and G. Printz-Påhlson—
headed down to Malmö and to Lund.
*Smultron's not the same as jordgubbe* said
a man in dark glasses sitting right behind us in
the Lane Arts Cinema, Columbus, 1959:
a handless clock, a coffin falling from the hearse,
and top-hatted ancients walking to their
*jubeldoktor* honors, Borg having dreamed
his way from Stockholm, Sarah both his lost love
and late Fifties girl, just like my Susan, flirting
with the guys in the back seat, chewing on her pipe.
What did I know then of time, of memory, of age?
And who would watch a movie wearing heavy shades?
We looked behind us and he nodded in a formal way.
Göran, ten years my senior, was writing poems
in Malmö that von Sydow liked to read—*Max*,
as he called him, who spoke his Swedish very well
whether as a knight in *The Seventh Seal*
or there before us pumping gas in *Smultronstället*
or when reading Göran's poems to a
little group of connoisseurs. But Max doesn't
get it when the doctor says, mostly to himself,
*Perhaps I should have stayed.*
We didn't get it either, though we stayed—right
through the film, and trying very hard.
In twenty years I'd introduce my friend from Skania
to my Midwest as Dr. Printz-Påhlson, poet.
A colleague thought that Göran was a royal and
called him Prince. Oh, and Göran hated
Bergman films, all that religious angst, which

everybody asked about, even though his lecture was
on Strindberg. So much for the 80s.
In 1959 Bibi Andersson was twenty-two, only
three years older than my girl friend.
I thought how much I'd like to sleep with her.
The man in sun glasses put his head between us
and said, *Place of wild strawberries*;
the English doesn't get it. The car drove on.
Years after Göran got his own degree at Lund, his head
literally belaurelled, little girls in white
throwing flower petals in his path,
he fell all humpty-dumpty down a flight of stairs
and broke his crown on the concrete, and lost
his sight, and pushed aside his work, and rests
in silence in a Malmö nursing home. With whom
share a joke, a plate of herrings, bog myrtle schnapps?
The nightmare examiner had said:
*You are guilty of guilt*
when Isak Borg mis-diagnosed his patient, saying
*She is dead. You are incompetent*, concluded the
examiner, and all of us got back into the car
and headed south: Borg & Marianne; Sarah, Anders, Victor;
Susan, John, & Göran; and the man in heavy shades.
The summer sun is blinding, even in the night.
*Smultronstället*. Wherever we were from,
we couldn't stay.

# Oscar

Not the movies, poems—
And before the days of Dons Allen and Hall.
Oscar Williams: pocket paper books
Of modern verse. (Also Little Treasuries.
Also Mentors and—revised—the Palgrave.)
Held now in contempt or just forgotten, Pocket
Modern was the Bible of my teenage faith.
"More than 500 Great Modern Poems"
Bulged in my pocket like a wallet stuffed with cash.
There was the Genesis:
Emily, Walt; there was the Exodus: poets still
In their prime.
         Those summers I worked
For minimum wage
At the State Auditor's office, Columbus,
I loved best what I least understood.
My blood pulsed pizzicati
When I smuggled lines of Wallace Stevens
In reports I typed. Entirely by the numbers,
Ohio's new electric Royal
Hopped to dollars & sense in the tables
I prepared—tabs
Jolting me over the page: tens and
Twenties and thirties of things; hundreds
And thousands and millions. If money was a kind
Of poetry, was poetry a kind of money too?
$2, 384, 958. 00—*A violent order is disorder; plus*
$3, 179, 265. 00—*A great disorder is an order.*
*These two things are one.*
No superior collecting my reports
Seemed to notice a thing, so I kept it up
All summer long. Stevens' Oscars
Bled into the numbers, then took over like
A sense of slight-of-hand,
Like *tootings at the weddings of the soul.*

Pool-side and lake-side, myself
I sang for Susan where in slim adolescence
She did all but strip as Yeats's music fell from
Pan's disco's Delphic oracle and we saw goat-head,
Breast, bikinied bottom in the pages of a book
Dedicated, 1954, to
*The Memory of Dylan Thomas—*
*Major Poet, Great man, Immortal Soul.*
Thirty pages of the Great Man.
Fifteen pages of George Barker; ten of Oscar
Himself; one of the other Williams, W. C.;
None of T.S.E. (who offered none,
Thinking, I discovered later, that my
Much revered anthologist was self-serving, vain).
In what vein was Auden's *Pray for me*
*And for all poets living and dead* (?)
*For there is no end to the vanity of our calling* (?)
I skipped that at the time and flew with hawk
And helmeted airman: *Beckon your chosen out* (!)

The chosen still included: Masters and Bridges,
Masefield, Lindsay, Wylie, Waley
Houseman, Muir, Millay, &
Frederick Mortimer Clapp. By the time I'd
Sanded fifty pages like a deep valley
Cut through mountains when my Harvard book bag
tied onto the luggage rack of the motor bike
I rode those days fell and
Was dragged half the distance from Mountain View
To Stanford, many an Oscar was maimed.
*Find also in the sou        ought*
*Hearing it by         sea*
*The sea*
*Was                    earth's shore*
Even Matthew Arnold still was Modern—
*Dover Beach* an Oscar there between the Civil War

Of Melville and *Mikado's Song*.
The last poems, unsanded, were intact; the last line
with a confident finality declares:
*The page is printed.*

# Don's Drugs

I read that teenage girls
Routinely send out naked pictures
Of themselves to boy friends
And even strangers on the Internet.
And then I think about my own
Generation of kids, staring only
At the movie magazines
In shops like Don's. We'd get
Our cherry cokes there too, and
Sometimes even have prescriptions
Filled. There was Marilyn, even Betty,
Though a little old; there was young
Liz Taylor—all in rather proper
One-piece bathing suits. We'd pretend
To be reading *Road and Track*, even
*Classic Comics* where I had
My first encounter with Shakespeare.
Ballooning out of Caesar's mouth—
*Et Tu, Brute*? What ballooned from
Half opened mouths of movie
Stars? (We never thought to wonder
What might enter them.)
Don would lurk about, watching
From behind the soda counter
With its five round stools you could
Spin when you got up to leave. Although
Eventually I owned the whole series
Of *Classic Comic Books*,
I remember best the movie mags I never
Bought. Marilyn! Betty! Liz!
*And you, Brutus*? Even he was headed
Through the aether toward those girls born
As we approached a *fin de siècle*.
Out there somewhere all of them,
Blooming & ballooned, are
Tangled in some lonely virgin's
Pixellated dream.

## Ned's Sister, Pete's Dad

My neighborhood was pretty much divided
Between streets that crossed a hundred yards
Or so beyond the entrance to my drive:
Ned's street, out and to the right, or—
Out and to the left—Pete's. Although these
friends were neither Swanns nor, certainly,
Guermantes, they split my world in two.
And though I didn't know it then, part of
That division had to do with class. Ned's father
Didn't seem to be around, and his mother
Worked all day at the local five and dime.
His sister was in charge of him. Pete's father
Was Professor of pathology, School of Dentistry,
Ohio State University, Columbus. He'd line up
Slides for lectures on the family dinner table.
Knowing I got queasy when I saw them,
He'd laugh and hold one up and say, *Now
That's pathological! Watch out whom you kiss.*
I was twelve and hadn't kissed a soul.
But Ned's sister was fifteen and clearly had.
Pete claimed he'd kissed a girl once, down the
Road that led to Old Glen Echo Park.
His father held his slides up to the light.
Even now when I hear someone jesting—*Now
That's pathological*—I see diseased mouths,
Lesions on the lips, inflammation of the epiglottis,
Sets of toothless gums, bleeding and infected,
Or, most frightening of all, tongues already
Half cut away, maimed organs of speech.
He'd go to his class and flash these on the screen
With the keen enthusiasm of an art historian
Dissecting a Giotto. Ned's sister, I imagine, had
Already been debauched. I was once allowed
To take her picture in a bathing suit. She'd put
Things in her mouth, suck a mixing spoon
All full of icing for a cake. Ned would shout

Out *gross*, a word ruined by its use in situations
Just like this, as later *awesome* would be ruined
And recently, borrowed from the English, *brilliant*.
Was the slide I took of Ned's sister in her
Bathing suit and sucking on a spoon *brilliant*,
*Awesome*, or *gross*? Maybe it was all of these.
My parents didn't like me spending time
With Ned and his sister. They'd talk up Pete
Enthusiastically: *A boy that's bright and has*
*A future. Ned's not the kind of friend for you*
*To have.* When I'd mention anyone at all I'd met,
One or the other of them asked: Who's he?
They meant: Who is his father? I think Ned's father
Was a wino out of work, but then I only saw him
Once or twice and he never spoke to me at all.
Pete's dad would say: *Don't start drinking alcohol;*
*It causes eight different kinds or oral lesions*
*And can scar the esophagus and give you*
*Duodenal ulcers.* I have no idea what became of Ned.
He disappeared one week at summer's end along
With his mother and his sister. Dog days.
The house was up for sale. Pete became a periodontist
And the head of his department at Northwestern.
When my colleague Conrad Schaum came back
to Notre Dame after having been to Pete for surgery,
he looked as if he'd had his upper gums sewn up
by a Singer, stitches beautiful and regular and tight.
*That friend of yours*, he mumbled as I poured him
Out a drink, *is pretty good*. I said: *You should*
*Have known his dad, who used to scare me half*
*To death.* I saw Ned's sister last a week or so before
The family left our neighborhood. She rolled back
Her head and said: *I bet you don't have guts enough*
*To kiss me.* Ned said *Gross!* And I thought *Awesome!*
*Brilliant!* (though I didn't know those words).
My tongue felt sick. But she had opened wide.

# Red Root's Spleen

      is always there among
"The pickled foetuses and bottled bones"
Which come to mind—those words attached
Like labels to a thought—whenever I

Smell alcohol, preservative, or just
Walk in for blood work at a lab.
Root was stabbed by a classmate and
Staggered down our high school

Hall, a switchblade in his abdomen.
It was an argument about a girl.
That afternoon, he nearly died in surgery.
Somehow the extracted organ ended up,

Like other curiosities, in alcohol, and
Labeled *Human Spleen*. He was
Last scion of the Blackboard Jungle days:
*Disfecemi Maremma*, or Ohio.

The dark back room of 321 Biology
Where all these things were kept
Was also where the sexually precocious
Locked themselves away at noon.

It was an underworld populated by the
Amputations, parasites, and parts that our
Magister collected. There they did
What daring would permit. Though squeamish,

I was asked to feed the snake its mice
And once to saw a monkey's head in two,
Spoon its brain into a little dish. *Blood, girls*,
The Magister declared: *liquor of initiation*

*In whatever rite or wrong.* His lab coat was
Spotted with red drops. I thought the spleenwort
Was a good idea for a Gnome who needed
Passage through a dismal place, or, sick of Paris,

For a syphilitic down with ennui to brandish
As he entered branching catacombs. Whose lock,
Rolled into a deed, concealed more of magic than
Our Caseous Mass in mason jar: *Trades—*

*though a foole be hurl'd spleen, shittle, cocke?*
We of course called Root himself "The Mandrake."
We called his spleen lymphatic, sinusoid.
We called each other, in exasperation, spores.

# Junior Brawner

Why the wrestling team, my father asked, shaking
His head in wonder. *Wrastling*! as he said it.
How could I admit that I wanted a high school letter so
My girl friend would sleep with me? And there
Was no one else in my weight class, so I'd get one
If I just showed up enough. Everything was going pretty well
Until we met the State School for the Blind. I'd even won
A match against a tall and scrawny kid from The Academy,
Our football rival. (We were the "University School,"
Deweyite, progressive, founded in the 1930s by some people
Who were hounded in the 50s by McCarthy.) The problem
With the Blind School was that they were really good; they
Wrestled all year long and were feared across the state. Once they
Had their hands on you your goose was cooked. Especially mine.
A week before the meet I heard a teammate saying, *I sure
Hope Brawner's gained or lost some weight this year. Last
Year I was in his class and what he did to me was so bad
I was taken straight off the mat to an ambulance. Now they've
Banned the hold he used that nearly broke my neck.*
Nervously, I asked the coach about this Brawner and he said,
*If you're not in luck he's slimmed down to 138.* I was
Not in luck. For a few minutes I thought I was. Two pounds
Over at the weigh in, he asked the ref to ask me to accept that.
I wouldn't do it. Standing on the scales he looked
As if he must be made of steel. His muscles rippled. He set
His jaw and mumbled: *Man, I'll go lose the weight.*
He had three hours before the match began. Holding hands
With an assistant coach, he ran eight times around the lake.
He put his finger down his throat, he took a laxative.
By four o'clock he'd somehow lost two pounds. And he
Was angry. I mean angry like Achilles. Like a creature who
Could tear your arm off sans compunction, drag you by the hair
Around the gym while you screamed and begged for mercy.
Hopefully, I'd asked my girl friend to show up for the match.
My parents too. He'd clearly asked his father—Senior
Brawner, I suppose—who looked just like him, but was sighted,

And whispered in his son's ear as he glared at me, things like:
*Junior, this guy looks just like a wimp, or Save your sweat
For the regionals.* It was suddenly time. I decided that
The better part of valor was to throw the match, take a dive,
Play possum, turn turtle, whatever. All unnecessary.
As I struggled to avoid his Beowulf-grasp, I somehow caught
Him with my elbow in the nose. He bled profusely, though
At first it wasn't clear where all that blood was coming from.
My heart, lung, kidneys, liver, brain? And now he went for me in
Real fury. Two points for a take-down. Then I felt his left
Arm under my arm-pit, hand on my neck, his right
Hand somehow grasping it from across my chest until my
Head was forced between my legs, butt in the air, shoulders
On the mat. Upside down, I saw the referee awarding the match—
To me! In his anger he had used the banned, illegal hold.
Disqualified! I stood there covered in his blood, victorious.
The coach came out and shook my hand. My father looked proud.
My girl friend whispered in my ear—*Tonight!*
*But not in that position.*

# Walking Adagio: Indoor Track

She passes at a trot and says
As she goes by, *Hi There Prof!* She's
Got her iPod plugged in her ear.
I have a Walkman playing
Mahler, but can read her lips.
Her running shorts are nearly
Transparent, her young
Breasts bounce. She assumes
We do not notice, here in
The middle lane. On the inside
Geezer lane, the real Senior Cits—
Guys on walkers, poor men dragging
Stroked-out legs, an onset Alzheimer
Or two. I toddle on. *Adagio,
Adagio* says Mahler. *Sex
And rock* her iPod doubtless blares.
Round and round. Would she
Care if she saw me staring at her ass?
An old friend, days before retirement,
Was brought before a board by
Someone who objected to his
Saying *Pussyfoot* in class.
Would I dare affirm before some
Academic court: *No teaching
Without eros*? I affirm it here.
And no learning either. I think
Of the absurd charge against
My friend, and then of our shared
Old school, girl friends, jazz,
And cars. We didn't pussyfoot around.
Mahler says, *Forget it pal—that
Was long ago.* Hayfoot, strawfoot,
Left and right. At least I still
Can walk. Now she comes
Around again, running like the
Future wasn't here.

# Late Elegy for Anthony Kerrigan, Translator

And at your funeral, two wives. Only you could
Bring that off with style: the young one wearing
Widow's weeds and playing it as theatre, the
Other—"real wife" as many old friends said—
At the back with all your handsome sons: Did mother
Church embrace this innocent & cheerful bigamy?
Did you lie down Lamech there, your Zillah
And your Adah looking on?
                              Best of all,
I liked the story about how you got
Your house in Mallorca. At a restaurant bar in Cannes
You'd met Picasso, who drew on all
The napkins while he talked. Half the night he talked.
Half the night he drew, and surreptitiously you
Gathered up the napkins. He drew on the menu,
The placemats, the backs of magazines. You swept
Those up as well. When Picasso stood
To leave, you said: "Maestro, will you sign
All these drawings for me *por favor*?" He glared
At you, then laughed, then signed. Deposited to
Age like wine or securities, they came out of
The strong box some years later & were translated
Into the Mallorca house where Borges
Was the guest of Lorca's *Duende* & your compadre
Cela's Pascual Duarte dined on Unamuno's
Tragic Sense of Life. Your own undiminished
Sense of life favored comic incongruity. Sitting
By me at a solemn convocation once, you
Shouted out of total boredom: "VIVA FIDEL!"
Turning to the nun on the other side of you &
Growling—"Sorry, Sister, I can't help it, it's A BAD
CASE OF TOURETTE'S & I have to shout out things like
FUCK THE POPE and UP THE REVOLUTION"—you,
The only Irish-Cuban anti-Communist translating
Japanese torpedo manuals in the war
To lose his commission suddenly for having been,
For just about three days in 1938, a Trotskyite.

But the funeral. I said to William:
"Tony would have really loved this crazy afternoon."
And William: "Oh, I'm sure he does."

# 1969: Moon, MacDiarmid, Apollo

He was old and deaf and angry still.
I'd come to get some poems
for an anthology. "Professor!"
he said—and was he mocking me?
I was only twenty-eight & didn't
like professors; I thought myself
a poet, just like him. My wife
was even younger, called Diana
for the moon. That very night
a man from Apollo walked up there—
on the same yellow moon that lights
the thistle's metamorphoses in
Hugh MacDiarmid's poems.
The three of us went out together
in the dark: No one thought he
saw the man from Apollo. "Professor!"
said MacDiarmid. I said "Mr. Grieve!"
(which was his name), doubting the
propriety of *nom de plume* in casual
conversation . . .
        Diana whispered
in my ear: "Does moonlight
make him Grieve, or is that just the man
in the MacDiarmid?"

# Poetics

*for Kevin Ducey*

Kevin says he's reached a second stage, a real "after" that
He favors over the "before" which might be illustrated by
Comparison with Barnett Newman's abstract painting "Canto IX."
The "after" Kevin says is, on the other hand, very like the
"Odalisque" by Robert Rauschenberg—the issue being
Do you leave the chicken in or take the chicken out.
The Rauschenberg I get: There's the chicken on the top,
About to lay an egg. But though there isn't any chicken in
The Newman, the same could be said of many works, or even most.
And who knows, there may be a chicken hiding underneath
What Kevin calls Newman's "pop art sheen," now painted out.
Or even a rooster, crowing away. So I have trouble with "before."
My friend Jerry, another poet, says that although he likes
Most of Kevin's "after" poems, he disagrees with the
Chicken Manifesto that's brought forward to explain them.
When he lived on his parents' farm, he tells me, his job
Was to go out in the evening and collect the chickens from
The trees they'd flown up into, grab them by the legs, and put
Them back in the coop. He says he likes the chickens where
They belong. That's not to say that he favors Newman's
"Canto IX" or Kevin's early poems. Not at all. He just disagrees
About The Chicken, and its place in poetry. So did his student once:
He was teaching that Williams poem you've thought of already
And the student said he hated it. Why such vehemence about such
A modest poem? He said that he, like his teacher, had grown up on
A farm & hated chickens, that he didn't want a chicken in a poem.
Unlike Jerry, he also didn't want it in a coop, but entirely out
Of mind. Besides he said, they've got the $H_5N_1$ flu and eventually
Will kill us all. He got quite worked up. Jerry quickly moved on
To Wallace Stevens. And once there was a family moving
Quickly on to Santiago, Spain. At an inn on the famed pilgrim route
A pretty maid flirted with the handsome son, who piously
Resisted her advances. Furious, she put a silver goblet in his
Travel bag which fell out with a clang as the family left.
Thief! cried the innkeeper, summoning the magistrate. Alas,
The handsome boy was taken out and hanged. But *mirum*!

While his parents trudged on in their pilgrimage, angels held him
In the air for weeks, his feet just off the ground, the rope loose around
His neck. When they returned to the inn, the hanging boy shouted
*Father! Mother! Take me down, I live.* A woman ran to tell the
Magistrate who was just about to eat a chicken for his lunch.
The boy lives, she cried. Nonsense, said the magistrate, *he's no
More alive than this chicken on my plate*—which came to
Life, and flapped its wings, and flew away. So did the angels
Flap their wings, and flew straight up to heaven.
So when the artist came to paint the miracle, there was not
A single winged creature to be seen.
         And Kevin—
He's writing some new stuff. He sends me an e-mail
Wondering what to do with a fox he's seen walking near his poems.
It's a third phase, I tell him. Admit the fox.
But be careful of the farmer there behind the tree
Who holds a gun.

# Another Movie, Colonel B.
*Remembering Ian Watt*

What they whistled wasn't Malcolm Arnold, 1957,
But Kenneth Alford, 1914. And yet that year after Suez,
Arnold sued a record company for marketing
A march in which the whistle morphed into his own
Counterpointed composition, flutes and drums
And horns celebrating fiction as the facts dropped away
And 1942 sweat out its guts in Technicolor
On a bridge across the wrong bloody river. Just ask
Your professor who had built the real thing and
Told you after twenty years that Jósef Korzeniowski,
Sailor, wasn't an Imperialist. He also told you
He himself awakened once thinking about Conrad's grave
In Dover—why no mention of his wife? Strange
That a starving POW in Thailand would be worried
About that. Might as well go out and watch a movie; might
As well go whistle in descending minor thirds. Bogey did
Exactly that instead of shouting *Fore* when he hooked
His drive. The hidden bird up so high outside my window
That I can't see him now for all the leaves and sun isn't
Shouting *Fore*. He too likes to whistle in descending thirds.
*Ti-Dee, Ti-Dee*, he sings. *Hi-ro. Hi-to*. His news is
Out of date for heaven's sake. It's 2007 but these musics
Stir a counterpointed theme. I squeeze a girl's hand as a
Train chugs through the jungle toward the cantilevered artifact
An English Colonel loves, sabotaged by other Brits.
Six years later and I'm in the Stanford office of my teacher
Talking fiction. What are facts? What are railway tracks
Running all the way from Bangkok to Rangoon?
The real thing. The hammering of iron spikes rang with a
Reason for the working party on a slick embankment.
He could hear it still. What I heard along with what he said
Was Malcolm Arnold's take on Alford's Limey tune; what
I saw was lifted up by hired Danish engineers in Thai
Ceylon across a stretch of river unremarked on any map.
They'd mastered the resistance figures and the coefficients,
Knew the depths to which the piles needed to be sunk.

When the bridge is finished there is cabaret, applause—
A celebration where the weary Brits congratulate
Themselves at complicated intervals: 14, 42, 57, 63—
Multiply them each by each and find their roots.
The boots of all the men who worked had rotted off their feet.
The river valley was as dark as an entire continent in
Joseph Conrad's heart. What did Ian Watt care about
The grave of Jessie C in Dover as he starved in Thailand,
Talked to me in 1963? What? I kissed the girl and missed
The great explosion, bridge and train plunging in a Kwai
They'd found for movie moguls threading through
A lush jungle in which William Holden, Yank who
Outmaneuvers Alec Guinness at his game, escapes. Jessie C
Wanted an elaborate marble monument outlasting all
The sales of her husband's books; hence her
Name was missing on Korzeniowski's simple stone.
Colonel Bogey only wanted not
To hook his drive; Malcolm Arnold wanted credit for his march
Derived from Alford's take on Bogey's whistle, music
Worth an Oscar and the royalties from
Hyperdrive, The Breakfast Club, and MasterCard
Whose adverts started off in minor thirds like
Claims for territory made above me by the hidden bird.
On your Internet connection you can book
A 13:20 train from Bangkok which will cross the right river
On the wrong bridge in the least time. Just past Kanchanaburi.
The man who'd write a book about the book I'd read
The night before in 1963 had wanted to survive forced labor
Still alive and write it. He nearly died. He wanted
In a long digression just to make me see the travesty of
Honor, work and order represented by the monument a
Fictive English officer had caused to be
And toward which all the singing and the whistling rose.
My own hand I wanted on my pretty girl's breast.
So what's the test? Blacklisted writers had their names
Erased from screens while on the scrim of history

A script was beamed for ministers & patrons, dignitaries—
Wives and pretty daughters wearing Ascot hats—
Who'd come out from the capital to see the blast . . .
Which capital? The last before the failed coup or latest
Occupation anywhere, Bogey's whistlers listing for a hunt,
A hint of fame, a name put up in lights. The nights in fact
Brought nothing but despair and total dark, Conradian.
The last shot's the bridge in ruins taken from
A helicopter rising in the sky like music or a poet's lark
And flying on toward Vietnam. Mistah Watt—he was
Annoyed by that, whose bandog-days hadn't lost their bark.

# Little Elegy
*For James Robinson, Scholar*

Embolism, mitral valve, and then
a third surgery that didn't work.
And so our sub-Beckett dialogues
were done . . .
          Back the first two times
and hard at work on *Lear* . . .
he heard, he said, the voice of
death itself . . . *pray you undo this button* . . .

Brothers in the trade, moans &
groans exchanged across the hall
for years, we'd bitch with writer's
block while blockage in his
arteries beguiled him . . .

watching
rain on week-ends when we had
the building to ourselves: *My umbrella's
in the car. And mine.
Pray you, are there no more umbrellas?*

What he loved was baseball
and I think The Cardinals were his team.
They kept the life-support
machinery turned on until the whole
family had arrived.

Astonished doctors heard the
oldest son begin—*Take me out to
the ball game*, &
all the others joining in . . .

*Peanuts . . .*
*                    crackerjacks*
*I don't care if we never get back*
*don't care         ne*

*ver   ge*

*t back*

# A Douglas Kinsey Monotype

Diana gave me this the morning of our
Anniversary—the 20th—before the year when
She believed I had been lost to madness.
A young man with a black beard
Is lying on a bed. He looks like me
At twenty-five. A woman bending over him
Gestures with her arm. Kinsey has
Done something with the arm I can't explain,
Some trick with paint and printing
That has turned the gesture of the arm
Into an open sweep of brilliant wing.
That January I was suddenly ill. Everything
Went dark, and for many months I simply
Lay in bed trying not to think. The woman
By the young man's bed was always there,
Exasperated, hurt, pitilessly loving him.
*Get up*, she said. *For God's sake get up!*

# Arrangement in Gray and Black
*For Marjorie Kinsey*

Back from what Douglas said might be your *last*
trip to Europe, you laughed with a restrained
enthusiasm for the things you'd done yet one more time
and quipped: *Standing in the Louvre
I realized I'm older now than Whistler's mother . . .*
Doug and I, of course, that old as well—
all of us who made those
*first* trips to Europe, still by ship and slow
and full of time to spare in
that last year of Eisenhower, hoping that some utter
transformation might occur
just by setting foot on foreign soil.
Too much Henry James, too much Whistler,
too much Ezra Pound . . . ?

who wrote in 1912 ('To Whistler, American,' uncollected
until 1949) *You who tested, pried and worked
In many fashions! good for us to know*, he thought,
*Who bear the brunt of an America
And try to wrench her impulse into art*, but
somehow had to be
abroad, abroad, or heading there
aboard some ship or other like *The Rotterdam*
from which I disembarked in June 1960, still uncertain
just which Henry I should be, James or Miller.

Now I think of William Howells in Whistler's garden,
his transformation into Lambert Strether,
ambassador of *The Ambassadors*, the man who hadn't
lived, urging someone else to *Live all you can! Live all you can!*
What was the common household object that the
Newsome family made? You and I should be able to guess,
both of us from *nouveau riche* Columbus—next
stop after Winesburg—Ohio.
Have we lived all we might have, all we possibly could?
A thought worth thinking as we settle into poses,

getting stiff, and clutching
something in our laps, propped in straight-back chairs.
*I lifted up my heart that it might be cast down*
said Mrs. Whistler, sitting to her son. And this: *Jemie
had no nervous fears in painting me* . . .

                              Across
my living room from Doug's monotype
of the woman who'd arouse a poor man from despair
is his painting of the two of us, along with
a student, all collaged together
with a cello leaning on a chair.
In the background, people are embracing.
I am reading poems. You are looking down at something
in your hands. We're still young—at any rate,
we're not yet old. Somehow Whistler, James and Pound
got us from Ohio to Abroad.
The old magic places, the ambitions of youth,
gardens, galleries, glitter of the stories read and told—
bright arrangements of the many dancing colors,
turning imperceptibly to black and gray.

# Tsunami: The Animals

Not very many animals died. The human beings, sucked
Out of their windows, plucked from one another's arms, may
Have heard the trumpeting of elephants, may have seen
Flamingos group and leave for inland forests, boars and
Monkeys heading for a higher ground. Do even fish that
Swim in grand aquariums of restaurants where we eat
The flesh and organs of clairvoyants on some $87^{th}$ floor
Detect the tremor we don't feel until we crash through
Ceilings in a fall of rubble upside down, a fork impaled
In an eye? Are the creatures then an ark? Noah, no one knows.
Does the trunk laid flat upon the earth before a trumpeting
Begins detect an earthquake or tsunami in the human heart
As well as movement of tectonic plates, approaching footsteps
Of a man who'd rather be a bomb? A flood, a flash of
Detonation. Caged canaries in our common mine
Burst through bars in song. High in heaven's Yala,
Water buffalo are shaking off the waters of the world's woe.

---

Yala: An animal preserve in Thailand

# Column I, Tablet XIII

*(For Gilburt Loescher, UN High Commission for Refugees)*


. . .

mostly broken, but assumed to be
a lone survivor . . .
                         . . . man called Gil
is what the paper said
if you were able to decipher the Akkadian,
cuneiform . . .
             A man called Gilgamesh,
was king and had a friend.

Climb along the outer wall, the inner wall,
study the foundation . . . . . .
expedition . . . dream
in a nether world. Apsu, the abyss

He lived next door to me for many years
and he would read beneath the tree that shaded
both our gardens. Tall Gilgamesh, he'd
play basketball with local kids and let them win.
His friend Sergio called to him
from Baghdad. Man of peace, scholar
of our failure to mend . . . he went . . .

in schools they studied exorcism . . .
Sîn-Lequi-Unninnī wrote it down. Humbaba came
the outer walls collapsed . . . inner walls

his wife Ann doing her *tai chi*
as Gil read on, then stringing wire between
our houses, hanging up a feeder for
the yellow-throated finch

Gil hanging upside down in rubble
by his broken legs, calling

for his friend. Terrible the flash of light
O terrible the thunder-blast

column... tablet... Enkidu

# Guy Davenport's Tables

. . . and what thou lovest well
Will probably be reft from thee.
I never met Guy Davenport but sometimes
We would talk for hours on the phone—
David Jones, Stanley Spencer, Doughty's
Strange *Arabia Deserta*, Ezra Pound.
He once said he feared the best of it would be
Forgotten. He hated cars and always
Walked to teach his class. When computers
Took us over, he stuck to his Hermes.

I hadn't heard that he was ill, but when
A friend told me following a visit that a book
Of mine was coffee tabled chez Davenport, I
Fairly swelled with pride. A place of honor!
Better there than in the British Museum,
The library at Alexandria, or carved in stone.
But pull down thy vanity! He said he knew
His own work would die. People had forgotten
How to read. And how to walk. And how
To write a letter to a friend they'd never met.

He himself was soon lying on a table in his
Own school's anatomy lab. Like Whitman, he
Loved the body and the natural things it does
And can reveal to the mind. But I pray that the
Student whose cadaver he became in Lexington
Didn't recognize the face he had to cut away, the
Keen eyes gone dark, the mouth and tongue
That spoke good words. Like Old Ez at Pisa,
Guy had folded up his blankets. Eos nor Hesperus
Had suffered wrong at his hands—

His last letter to me signed in fun, *Erwhonian*.

# Walter's House

(Passing on the Campion, for Cornelius Eady)

I know it's Walter's house no longer,
But I think of it, because I've thought of it
That way for thirty years and more,
As Davis Place. For far too long it was
Entirely empty. When I was young and just
Had come to town, he welcomed me,
Passing on *The Works of Thomas Campion*
He'd edited that very year, 1967.
It was the year I married. It was a year
When one could still persuade oneself
That the Sixties, whose veterans now are sixty,
Might in fact still usher in Aquarius by way
Of a machinery concealed by some Inigo
Within the fantasy of its extraordinary masque
Performed in Caesar's court...

        *From our house to yours,*
The inscription reads, *with hopes*
*For every kind of harmony forever.* I'd sit there
In his study imitating gruff Yvor Winters
Gruffly reading *Now Winter Nights,* and claim
That I had Stanford friends—Pinsky,
Hass and Peck—who had written poems already
That would matter. He drank too much,
Like Winters, and he told me in his cups
The price he'd paid for scholarship, the expense
Of spirit and the loss of years in dusty rooms
And half-lit archives. But his study was ablaze
With light and insight.

                When winter nights enlarged
The number of their hours, I'd walk South Bend's
Park Avenue and wish it were New York's.
Sometimes very late, one or two a.m., I'd pass his house
And see the beam across the snow from where his
Curtains didn't meet. He was still up and working.

First at his desk, then at the harpsichord, the Gamba,
Picking out an aire, testing theory against meter against
Song—*Goe, numbers, boldly pass*—with speaking voice
And then with instruments . . . In 1600 there went forth
From Campion a treatise where, he said,
It was "demonstratively proved" that
Quantitative counting was not cant in English.
Walter loved the massed sounds of strophes all full
Of l's and e's and o's, or lines all keyed to single
Vowel: *O then I'le shine forth as an Angell of light*.
He played through scales in tetra chords, listened
For the semitones, and anchored counterpointing
With the bass. *Nympha potens Thamesis*
*Soli cessura Dianae* raised her head above the ice
Of Campion's Latin verse. The Thames
Was the St. Joseph River, and the lady listened with me
In the night. She counted quantities
But looked like Bessie Smith. We thought we heard

A new music in that house that for so long
Was still. A poet filling up the walls again with books,
The study as a student of the word & song.
Among the maskers linger ghostly Lords like Scrope & North,
But Counts like Basie, Dukes like Ellington, emerge.
The innovative chords are Monk's.
When we walk along the street at night
We think we hear the lute of Muddy Waters
And Chicago Blues . . .

      Cornelius, I thought I'd
Pass on Thomas Campion because he lived so long in
Walter's mind who lived so long where you've arrived,
Bringing with you poetries to make a madrigal
Of time and circumstance, contingencies
And synchronicity. Take what you've said—*a motion,*
*Gambling's pitch, holding back and laying out,*

*Slow-mo chop-time logic lifted up & then away that*
*You can sing.* Invite Walt Davis to the house warming
With his book of ayres, his sackbuts and his
Gambas and his viols . . . And then shine forth.
Then shine forth like Angels.

*O then shine forth like Angels of the light.*

# The Large Iron Saucepan

Seemed to hold the world—broken wooden
Handle, heaviness itself to lift,
Bringing all the soups, the stews, the food
Of childhood. In the winter I would
Breathe its steam to open up my throat, ease
My croupy cough, both of us, the pan
And I, underneath a sheet. In anger once
I threw it on the floor—there beside
The ice box, dripping water through its cracks,
That we used for years before we had a
Proper fridge. And there was always coal
In the coal bin.
                    I'd sometimes stare at it
As if it were a crystal ball. It had
A presence, a purpose, a plan. It would outlast
All the dogs and cats, the uncles and
The aunts, the parents and the children. This
Mere thing. This piece of iron. It seemed to summon
Ice man, milk man, grocery boy, someone
Shouting on the street about the Fresh Strawberries
In his little cart he had to sell. And sometimes
Cross-town cousins dropping in to play.
After fifty years it sits here on another stove,
Sits here in another town, one small relic
From the past. I boil water in it for the hint
Of iron that will flavor the green tea. Holding
The warm handle, I am four, six, nine years old.
Someone's telling me—*take care, don't spill,
That's heavy.* Even Crusoe had a large
Pan that let his new world finally be. If I
placed this on a hill, would "the wilderness
Rise up to it, no longer wild"? Once I took it with
Me on a back yard camping trip and built
A fire and cooked a meal and stared
Up at the sky all full of stars. I ate directly from
It with a wooden spoon. And on Sundays

We had Sunday Barley Soup, cooked all day—
A ham bone leaking marrow in the
Broth. We'd turn the radio to Sunday Programs,
Something like Jack Benny, and we'd eat,
Now and then telling one another what we planned
To do next week. We'd break up saltine crackers
In our bowls of soup. We'd eat.

# Missing Cynouai

*My daughter's heavier*... John Berryman, Dream Song 385

My daughter hasn't spoken to me now for years.
I don't know why. I'm sure there's a good reason.
She must be angry about something, but she doesn't say.
No letters and no calls. She's nearly thirty-three.

My mother won't speak any more at all, but I know why.
And I'm surprised I think about her almost every day.
I'm over sixty. She is—what does one say?
My father spoke up last when I was just my daughter's age.

I don't think he's angry any more.
He's very quiet though. What was it made him angry
For so so long? I'd like to ask him that.
And other things. I'm surprised that I think of him

Almost every day. I didn't used to think of him at all.
It seems to me I didn't think of him for thirty years.
I wish my daughter would pick up the phone and call.
Or write a letter. Or a card.

I saw her last at someone's funeral.
"At the funeral of tenderness," said Mr. Berryman,
Who was my friend. A while ago!
My mother had an injury that would not mend.

He signed his poem about his daughter for my daughter.
That was 1969 when she was one.
Some months later he himself was gone—
But where? The daughter heavier, the father lighter there.

She must be angry about something, but she doesn't say.
Daughters frequently are angry, but often
Only for a moment or a day. I think she knows her old address.
I'm not certain where she lives right now. I think she

May have married someone, but I'm not entirely sure.
I'd be glad to meet him if she has. And her.
I'm surprised that I think about her almost every day.
I'm over sixty. She is—what does one say?

People used to love the music of her name, say *Cynouai*
just to savor once or twice the pleasure of the sound.
I sing it silently and carry it, a heaviness,
Around, around . . .

Missing's neither having lost nor found.

# For My Last Reader

There were not many of you
To begin with. Nonetheless, I worked
with all the skill I could muster.
It probably wasn't enough.
Still, for a while, I felt as if I might be
In touch with people I'd never met—
An exhausted graduate student
Taking a break from the 16th century,
A nun here and there, a teenage boy
Who couldn't get a date, a bad poet
Who wanted to write like me.
It was a little community, a silent
Chat room where nobody spoke before
The computers took over for good.
But I never heard what they made of
It all. I was there and not there.
In the end they began to give it up:
The boy found a girl who would
Marry him, the nuns returned to Christ,
The grad student failed his comps
And took up crime, and the bad poet
Ceased to read altogether and only wrote.
And here you are—in the stacks
Of some stone memorial to the word
When books have been replaced
By strange machines as thoroughly
As oral poets were replaced by books.
Lord knows what you're doing there—
Curious, it may be, about the past,
Or possibly just lost. Only chance placed
Your hand on this particular book,
In which you read a few lines from one
Of the shorter poems and put it back
On the shelf, where it continues—
*Comerado, this was a man!*—
Moldering and moldering to dust.

# II

# The Memoirists

1—The Grocer
(Lorenzo da Ponte, *Memoirs*)

2—The Pirate
(Edward John Trelawny, *Records of Shelley, Byron and the Author*)

3—The Gondolier
(Frederick Rolfe, Baron Corvo, *The Desire and Pursuit of the Whole*)

4—The Housekeeper
(Céleste Albaret, *Monsieur Proust*)

5—Epilogue: Four Seasons of Vladimir Dukelsky
(Vernon Duke, *Passport to Paris*)

# The Grocer

I

                ... *C'est Emmanuel*, Beaumarchais had written
When Bortolo finds that Figaro's his long lost son.
But for Mozart, Da Ponte wrote "Rafaello!"
Suddenly, today, he thought of that. He wouldn't put
It in his book. So many years since he had been Emmanuel—
Emanuele Conegliano, tanner's son. And there were other things
He wouldn't write: about the ghetto in Ceneda, red berets,
Smells of the tannery, the real reason he was hounded out of Venice.


But he'd write about Metastasio, great Italian poet to the Caesar
In Vienna; and Ceneda's Bishop, Lorenzo the Magnanimous, who
Named him as a son and sent him to a seminary to become a priest.
But his true conversion wasn't to the Christ of the Serene Republic:
It was poetry, and music, and a life initially of dissipation and disguise
He loved. He'd only let his reader know the half of that—bring him
To the bed of lust and quickly drop the curtain or, like Cherubino,
Hide beneath a song inside his dress: *Quello ch'io provo vi ridirò*.


And improvise, as he did all through his life. Perfect meters, sonnets,
Terza rima, sung on any subject *ex abrupto* on demand, or as part of
An extemporized seduction. The Jewish Padre numbered conquests like
His own Don Giovanni yet to come, lived with pregnant Angioletta
In a brothel where he entertained the ladies reading Petrarch before mass.
A letter of denunciation was deposited anon. in the stone lion's mouth
At San Moisè. *Mala Vita* was the charge, and whoring priests were
Commonplace. Golden horns in declamations from Rousseau were not.

II

Did he have in mind the Doge? It was an exercise in rhetoric, a game
He'd set his students in debate where one maintained "that man, by
Nature free, by laws becomes enslaved"—and then alluded to
The *corna aurate*. Moreover, there was revolution in the air: America
Cast off the Brits; Figaro prepared to get the best of Count Almaviva . . .
*Cinque, dieci, venti, trenta* . . . and the Senate sent Da Ponte into exile
From La Serenissima after three Esecutori Contro La Bestisemmia
Held against him for his lechery. The Doge adjusted his horned cap.


In his travel bag, a poem for his friend Pisani. He'd quote that in
His book. And say that he was brought before Esecutori charged with
Eating ham on Fridays. No Angioletta, no priest's whore. He had
His Dante, his Horace & his Petrarch. And he'd still have in Austria
His bella figura too; he had it yet at sixty there in Sunbury, PA.
From his window he could see *the spectacle of one continuous garden
With quantities of wild laurel garlanding the roadsides.* (When he
Weighed the turnips & potatoes, he still imagined laurels on his brow.)


The mountain flanks figured on *both sides a rustic theatre: Rocks, cascades,
Of water, hillocks, cliffs, masses of white stone*—Not so picturesque
In winter. Twice he'd nearly died: tumbling from his wagon as the horses
Shied, broke loose, and tossed him on the road; and when, that same
Disastrous year, a stage he rode in out of Philadelphia slid off of an icy
Bridge and pitched him in the river underneath. Arranging rural produce,
Counting coins, he remembered reaching Hamburg once by coach along
The frozen Elbe and seeing broken wheels sticking up out of the ice.

III

Vienna! No Magistrate of Blasphemy lived there when Joseph fired
His mother's spies and cancelled pensions for the privileged who had
Served her reign, even Metastasio's, who died blaspheming from the insult.
Italian opera was restored—its gaiety, its comedy, its sprezzatura too—but
Also its intrigues & catfights among divas, lovers, commissars of culture.
After all the *secca* of the Classic seria, music asked for something new,
And somehow Mozart stumbled on Lorenzo, exuberant in exile, when his
Head was full of Beaumarchais. Joseph made him Poet of the Theatre.


Between his customers he wrote there in the little Pennsylvania town
About how a finale had to glow with genius and a certain special
Frenzy: *everybody sings and every form of singing must be part of it,*
*Adagio allegro the andante intimate harmonious and then the Noise*
*Noise Noise with everything in uproar and with everyone on stage in*
*Twos and threes and tens and sixties solos duos terzets sextets yet more*
*Noise and yet more uproar and excitement and intensity and drama*
*And the tutti and the drum beats stop the singers stop and it's the end.*


It ended all too soon. *Figaro* & *Giovanni*, *Così* flaming brilliantly in
Three bewildered cities, an astonishing five years, and then all that
Masonic gibberish by Schikaneder-Giesecke in ugly Deutsch guttering
like farts out of the maestro's lovely Flute. But his trilogy was there:
*Amor* it said & *Pace*. It said *Forgive, Forgive*. And know the limits of
Your love, the limits of forgiveness. His grand and human mass, O *Kyrie*.
His *Dies Irae* and his *Agnus Dei* from the lips that kiss and tell and
Lie but say *Perdono*. Mouths agape with song. God with us . . . Emmanuel.

IV

But not, perhaps, in Sunbury. Or Philadelphia. Where were all of
The Italian books—the poems, the songs? *Grapes, yes. Olive oil, yes.
Silk and marble, yes and yes. And yes rosolio and sausages and
Macaroni. Wine. Cheese from Parma. Straw hats from Leghorn.
But not one bookstore kept by an Italian*. He'd change all that once
He paid his debts. Settled lawsuits. Sorted out the troubles of his
Troubled son. It was Giovanni dragged down in the flames and not
Lorenzo. Mozart's *Requiem* just said *Despair*. He had no hand in that.


He'd not despair. And then his dissolute son Joseph came back home
From college with consumption. Lucky in his marriage, Lorenzo
Had an English wife with fortitude enough for both of them. He
Mourned and wrote and mourned and moved into the country with
*The Prophecy of Dante*, Byron's poem, for company. The first English
Terza rima, Byron thought. Lorenzo put it back into Italian and
Translation purged his grief: *Too raw the wound, too deep the wrong,
And the distress of such endurance too prolonged . . .*


He came back not to turnips but to Tasso, himself translated finally
To America as bridge to all the things in Italy he loved. No more grain
For the distilleries in Philadelphia or creditors confusing him with
Brandywine's Dupont: he'd cook his enemies in olive oil & sell them
All as hostages: Salieri, yes. Casti, yes. Count von Rosenberg, yes & yes
And yes. He'd launch his memoirs as assault by the insulted with the
Vehemence of Leperello's list in D: double it & double back to Venice
And Vienna, London and Ceneda: No more macaroni and straw hats.

# V

1823 and he publishes his book, Volume One of *Memoirs*. He's in
New York by now attracting students, known to men like Clement Moore
And Joseph Bonaparte, alias the Count of Survilliers. When his
*Discourse apologetico*'s exported, readers, literati and Italian dealers in
Consignment send him books—3000 in the end—delighted and surprised
To find him still alive. Eventually he fills his house & then his shop & then
The bookstores of Manhattan with Boccaccio and Petrarch, Dante, Casa,
Tasso, Ariosto—and teaches all his students how to read them well.


And then *Don Giovanni* comes to town. He's nearly eighty, still writing
Up adventures from his youth. His prose moves in Vienna as Vienna
In New York moves in his verse: Giovanni minus all the ancient quarrels
Of his chronicle; word and music in a city without memory. At least
Without his memory, although he can't stop telling tales, interrupting
Even this performance whispering into a neighbor's ear *That's my opera,
Friend, & he'd have never done it anyway like that without my play.
He was a genius, of course, but so was I. Lorenzo Da Ponte, poet!*


He scribbles on. He's eighty-six, he's eighty-eight, he's dizzy with
His work and thinks he's at the theater. Someone on the stage
Is pointing to him, saying: *C'est Emmanuel!* But no stone guest is
Stalking toward him. It seems to be Susanna, with her bridesmaids
Dorobella and Fiordiligi. Leperello says, *She's Lady Wisdom in a
Servant's dress; you knew that everything was a disguise from
The beginning.* Susanna whispers: *Emanuele, E questro, signor scultro—
That will teach you, rascal.* And he: *Perdono . . . cielo . . .*


*Laurel . . . garden . . . venti trenta mala vita pace & . . . my bride*

# The Pirate

I

                He'd been surprised to find Lord Byron happy
For a day. A translation of his Dante poem, chiming in Italian,
Had come into his hands in Pisa. It was the work of a Venetian grocer
Living in America who once had been a friend of Casanova's
And had made the play that Mozart set to music in his own *Don Juan*.
Trelawny didn't know much Mozart, but he feigned
Enthusiasm at the news hoping that his master-childe, his own Giovanni,
Might by this Da Ponte's poem be drawn out of a melancholic funk.


That was long ago when he used to fill them full of tales about
His early life at sea with the wholly fictional De Ruyter,
Privateer & mentor, & the cast of characters he blathered up right
On the spot when he saw that all of them—Byron, Shelley,
Mary, Claire, & all their circle—took his bluster for the literal truth.
They started calling him "The Pirate Tre." He loved it; in the end
It got around that he had been the model Lord B's Corsair.
That was long ago and now he was a farmer in the town of Usk.


He'd written down the tales he told those Pisan credulousi in
*Adventures of a Younger Son*. Egged on daily by the poet Landor,
Cautioned by the cautious Mary, he published his assault on fame
With a book proclaimed by some to be the greatest sea adventure since
*The Odyssey*. But for twenty years he'd farmed in Usk, married to the
Shadowy Augusta, father of three children, forgotten man of a Romantic
Age long past, planting cedar cones he'd gathered from the grave
Containing Shelley's ashes back in Rome . . .

II

Along with cedar cones, he had some bits of Shelley's bones, a piece
Of jaw, some fragments of the skull. And everybody soon would know
Just how he'd plucked the heart out of the fire and delivered it to Mary.
After twenty years of silence, he again began to write. His neighbors who
Had much admired his frugality & temperance, his heavy work on
His estate, even his austerity of manner & aloof deportment (although not
His laboring on Sundays or his naked bathing in the stream) hadn't heard
Of Shelley's pyre or what he found beneath the pall in Missolonghi.


He didn't tell the locals what he'd now tell all the world. He wouldn't
Offer them, as he later would Rossetti, a poet's relics or the
Shrunken heads of men whom as a privateer he had dispatched.
They only saw him digging in his fields, sowing seeds, playing with
His children, telling off his bailiff and receiving now & then an older
Daughter he called Zella—named for his child-bride in the *Adventures*—
Who came from Italy & swam with him, shameless too & laughing,
Dripping water from her breasts as she climbed up on the bank.


As he wrote his way into his past, the swagger from his early years
Returned. His Shelley was not Mary's nor his Byron Claire's.
He railed at both these women, dead or broken by the matter of
His book, but praised their youth, having kept his distance from them
As they aged—a florid novelist, a governess. Meanwhile there arrived
A girl in Usk, displacing Mrs. Tre. He wrote a friend that he had stuck so
In mud of Monmouthshire he feared to sink in it. He'd swim a mile.
He'd run for ten. He'd ride his horse careering down the coast.

III

For he was the Corsair, after all. While he was in America and still
On fire from writing the *Adventures*, they all had taken him on his
Outrageous terms, even charming old Da Ponte who had built by then
A New York opera house. Da Ponte told him that if he were young he'd
Make *Adventures* into a libretto, though he couldn't say for whom.
By now Trelawny could. Berlioz for sure—crazy and theatrical as he
Had been himself. He tried to swim the river underneath Niagara falls—
What, compared with that, was Byron's sidestroke at the Hellespont?


Not much. And yet he struggled back to shore, defeated by the rapids.
And then returned to England. And then became a farmer there in
Monmouthshire to bide his time, waiting twenty years to write this
Memoir, tough as he could make it. He'd not admit *Adventures* had been
Fiction, but this was something else. This was Byron's ravaged legs
Underneath his shroud revealed as extreme deformity and source of all
His work. This was Shelley as a radical and atheist, not as an insipid
Angel made up by Victorians. This was Klephtes on Parnassus.


For it was they who had occupied the muses' home and fought
For Greece—Odysseus Androutses, leader of this tribe. He'd arisen on
The mountain as if he were the fictional De Reuter brought to life, giving
Tre his sister as a child-bride who then gave birth to Zella, phantom lost
In Java flame & spice & ambergris, but now reborn. And the mountain
Fastness was their ship, Ulysses' claim on history, Trelawny's last
Romantic stand. Byron stayed behind in Missolonghi to negotiate with
British agents, Philhellenic volunteers, Ulysses' enemy Mavrocordato.

IV

And there he died, bled to death by leeches meant to cure his fever.
When Odysseus was murdered, Trelawny held the cave. And even then
People went on walking out of books as he had out of *The Corsair*,
Hope's *Anastasius* coughing up young William Whitcomb. Here was an
Assassin drunk on Hope as he himself was drunk on Byron, both gone
Native with their turbans wrapped about them and their pistols bulging from
Their silken belts—fictions breaking into lethal fact, and broken.
Whitman shot Trelawny in the back. Parnassus merely shrugged.


And went on manifesting the sublime. In Usk, Trelawny wrote about
*The elevation of a thousand feet above the plain, the rock face,*
*Projecting crags, the natural shelf of fractured stone, the great cave of*
*Galleries and chambers, vaulted roof. It was,* he said, *like a cathedral*
*When the softened light of evening or the moonlight made it glow.* A place
Where traitor Anastasius might drive The Corsair back to doggerel.
Trelawny advertised the sale of his ewes & lambs, Herefords & mules,
Plows and other implements, wagons & an excellent light gig, his house.


He had designed two poets' boats, and now he quoted in his book the
Letter Shelley sent him praising the *Don Juan*, not however mentioning
That builders had reduced the size from thirty to just eighteen feet
Or that Byron's *Bolivar* would have an iron keel, copper fastenings,
Roomy cabin, deck, & ability to weather storms. *Don Juan* got a false
Stern & prow, was schooner rigged, required a ton of ballast . She was fast
But dangerous and *we must suppose*, wrote Shelley, *that the name was*
*Given during sexual equivocation suffered by her godfather, Tre.*

V

Was Shelley killed by sailors thinking that milord Inglese was on board
*Don Juan* with his pots of gold? Easy to confuse two boats, two
English poets, one of whom had written something even Leghorn
Fishermen might know, title of it on the stern. *A dying man had told his*
*Priest that his felucca with its seven men, its pointed bow and lateen*
*Sails had rammed the undecked boat off Via Reggio. It sank at once*
*In heavy weather and the sailors could not get aboard.* Thus Trelawny
To *The Times*, quoted without comment in his book . . .


Which he revises in his mind sitting for his portrait by Millais. He knows
Where he'll be buried, having dug the hole himself so long ago
In Rome. Right by Shelley. Right where he had gathered cedar cones
He'd planted on his farm . . . Maybe he should even be more graphic
Writing of the dead in Dervenakia, *the riders still astride the skeletons of*
*Horses and the bleached bones of negroes' hands still holding ropes*
*Attached to camels' skulls.* He'd seen three palikars impaled, still
Alive, the stakes that skewered them exiting their shoulders near the ear.


Millais has asked him please to hold the young girl's hand—a model
Brought to play the role of child or muse—she might have been the sister
Of Odysseus, might have been the phantom Zella—and he sees his
Fingers turn to bone—in the mirror on the wall his head become a skull
And that in turn the cup from which Lord Byron drank. He feels a dizziness
Turning into something else, into something that Millais can't paint,
Something no Victorian will take from him, no leaded type or print contain,
No word or image capture, no fire on beach or balustrade consume . . .

# The Gondolier

I

>...*Gehenna of the waters! Thou sea-Sodom!*

That's what Byron wrote and that's what Baron Corvo
Found eventually. After he was Pope. After he was back as Fr. Rolfe,
The "Fr." really Frederick, though he'd have you take it
Plainly for the "Father" he had failed to become. But he had become,
Through machinations of his own, *Hadrian VII*! Why not be top dog
Among the cats, whether in original Prooimion bed-sit or in
The pedophiliac back streets and rank canals of La Serenissima?


Whoever else had written his own life in earnest as the Holy Papa—
Chosen through the failure of Scrutiny and Compromise when
Providence itself made his pontificate the bull by which he'd
Horn his own dilemma with a gaggle of electors hanging on his tail?
Rolfe, Corvo, Rose: these and other singers hymned a heteronymic
Troubled soul—caviar, said D.H. Lawrence, spooned from the belly
Of a living fish. Autofisher from an obstinate isle, he'd flash & grasp
Obscenely as the others cast; his the One & True & Apostolic net.


Neologistic, too. He found the common dictionaries quite inadequate
And added supplemental volumes of his own. Dr. Johnson
Of the weird invention, odd etymology, unexpected spell: *Prooimion*
His *proheme, proheim, proem*: word becoming flesh and flesh
Becoming word, his world reduced to bed-sit Y-shaped room or
Coffin-cradle gondola in which he rowed—*oh might well have rowed—*
Tadzio to Aschenbach in 1911, the true Waladzio to Thomas Mann.
*Proot proot* he shouted at his patrons who were mules.

II

For mules they were, his patrons, and he'd give them what they
Merited in the invective of *Desire and Pursuit*. He'd write
His memoir as *roman à clef*, treble boys singing the castrati parts
In his Venetian Vespers. Cleft foot and cases of the clap
Would summon him once he hove in view: Clemency was not
His dwelling place among the clerisy, and Flavio, his cat,
Was better company than men. If the priest Da Ponte masqueraded
As a Casanova, Corvo might affect the pilgrim and the pimp.


Pilgrim not to *Hadrian*'s Saint Peter's now. He sailed from his most
Eccentric book in topo, tacking in the Adriatic, musing on
The earthquake which was said to have been caused by the excess
Of eros in Venetian carnivals. His own vow of chastity had lasted
Twenty years, but only he himself and fiction's bishop-johnnies,
Owl-like hierarchs, had heard the call. His Vocation now in doubt, he
Sailed with his soul alone through winter seas, tsunami wave and
Blinding rain breaking on Calabria. Lights extinguished on the land.


In the morning of December 27, 1908, Crabbe discovers Zilda.
He searches for a cove by ruined villages and ties the topo to an oar
Driven in the sand. Hadrian VII now is Crabbe, Corvo is a sailor,
Zilda will be Zildo and then Zilda once again. Dead bodies,
Severed heads and limbs, lie all around. Zilda is descended from
A Doge: Falier Ermenegilda fu Bastian di Marin di Bastian di Marin
Is her name. She is a boy. He is a girl. Corvo doesn't know, but is
Frederick William Serafino Austin Louis Mary Rolfe . . .

## III

And pulls her from the wreckage of La Tasca, pulls him by
His heels from the pork-chop-bones, the wood-ash & the rags.
She has no breasts, but neither has he parts. A penis would resolve
An ambiguity even in the presence of a Doge. She'll be his
Servant; he'll earn his keep as second gondolier. Crabbe doesn't
Watch her change his sodden clothes and put on light. But then he
Stares: a creature in his world who isn't of this world, *a boy*
*By intention but a girl. Nature has been interrupted in her work.*


He writes it in his book. A book he thinks will either save
Or damn his soul. He comes about, sails back to Venice with his
Miracle. Zildo watches quietly. This aging man can struggle
With the boat all day and write all through the night. And what does
He write about? They agree that Z will be a boy for the eyes
Of Venetians and the English Colony and the Reale Società
Canottieri Bucintoro. He writes *I beg to apply for a situation as*
*A Gondolier.* He writes *The Desire and Pursuit of the Whole.*


Z warns Crabbe of winter storms, the wake of passing
Steam boats that can swamp the pupparin in which they'll sleep
Now the topo's sold. They ply the waters, unlicensed boatmen.
They swim together in the great Lagoon. Crabbe writes his tirades
Cribbing Corvo's letters to the men who helped him after
The assassination of the Pope he had become. His friends would
Kill him once again, encourage him to starve, watch him freezing
In a gondola tied up at nights to a crumbling palace wall.

IV

He denounces Benson to the bishop, names him Bonson
In his book; he denounces Pirie-Gordon ("Caliban") to publishers,
Taylor to Society of Law. *I have not slept or changed my clothes
In fifteen nights. In the fortnight I've had four lunches, two dinners,
Three breakfasts, teas at the Bucintoro club where I gobble all the
Crusts the members leave behind. Toad-eater and most cretinous
Of men, I offer you the sixty rats I've trapped since Monday last.
I offer you my bitterest execrations, former friend.*


He promises to write pornography and publish it in Pirie-Gordon's
Name. He'll put his patron's arms on the cover by authority
Of Sanctissima Sophia. Z finds him boys among the tyro gondoliers
And Corvo offers them to well-connected men in London who
Will pay him for a connoisseur's advice. He describes in letters lewd
And rare lascivious acts, the special skills of Z's young friends,
But doesn't put this in his book. *Sea-Sodom, Sea-Sodom*: Rocking in
His boat and writing with his large fountain pen in colored inks.


He's acquired his rules of punctuation reading Addisson. Punctual
As always, he meets the German for a journey to the Lido.
The German is a maestro celebrated by the world. He himself is
No-man, No-man, but Z is holy light. *Deus in adjutorium
Meum intende . . . me festina . . .* Monteverdi's Vespers, 1610,
Echoes from St Mark's. *Dixit Dominus . . . until I make thine
Enemies thy footstool.* No, he has no license but he knows from
Z what Herr Professor Meistersinger doesn't know he wants.

V

Corvo wants the recognition he deserves, wants his books
In print, wants his former friends to pony up their patronage,
Wants what Crabbe desires—*Tou holou oun tei epitumiai
Dioxei eros onoma*—To be whole in love. The old Duchess
Sforza-Cesarini might have loved him once, gave at any rate
A title to him and a small estate. And his "special friends"?
All turned against him. All to be assassinated in his book.
Who'd suppose from *Hadrian* he'd seize on the *Symposium*?


Crabbe staggers in the cemetery on the isle of Sanmichele.
He brings his gifts. This is where they bury strangers like himself.
White chrysanthemums and rose buds for an English engineer,
A baby in the columbarium. It's the Day of the Dead in Venice;
Earth a flooded ossuary now. He goes back to his boat, lies down
On his back while chanting *Kyrie eleèson* to himself, the waters
Rocking in response: . . . Then the black light, then . . . *che ragion
Tu ne hai aver 'l amante e no verdelo mai* . . . Zildo singing, Zilda's


Blood dripping from her arm: *Scusie, Sior, but I found you dead
And fed you ikor and you live*—lives like another who will die
Inside himself until he steps upon uneven paving stones in Paris
And the Venice of his youth floods into him like
Combray had done when he sucked from the madeleine mere tea
As if it were the blood of all his past—*you live*!
Though Corvo died, seeking to be Zildo's catechumen,
No mere Pope, no Hadrian, no liege of Sforza-Cesarini or Guermantes.

# The Housekeeper

I

          Lac Léman, he'd said. And told her that was where
Lord Byron and Madame de Staël had stayed, where
He had first got something right about unconscious memory. He'd
Ended one book there in order to begin the great unfinished one
That she was part of, that everyone he'd known was part of,
That would in the end restore the works of time in place
Of places that at first appeared to wash them all beyond recall like
Ripples from a boat across Geneva's lake . . .


At least that's what she thought he'd said. This man Belmont
Again had asked her to explain what she'd explained
Already. It was, she saw, a kind of test. He'd ask the same question
Several times and watch her closely. Once again she'd answer
As she had before. *Lac Léman*, she said he'd said. *And suddenly
Sensation of congruence & a joy altogether inexplicable until the ripples
From a boat converge from memory's Beg-Meil* & she says *Time it's
Time for you to g*o and he says *Sodomite certainly Monsieur*


*As everyone but you maintains* and she says *No I would have known
Since I knew everything and anyway you've asked me this
A dozen times.* She has her tests for him as well. Who is he, after all?
A friend of Henry Miller, the American pornographer. Monsieur
Has now been dead for sixty years. Do the young read Henry Miller in
Translations by Belmont? He uses words Monsieur would never
Want to see in print. Nor would she, a woman over eighty—but not
Without desire. For the truth at least, spoken into a machine.

II

That whirs like Krapp's last tape. Georges Belmont has told her
About Beckett and his play in which an old man speaks into a little
Microphone reciting memories of his past like she does now—Beckett
Yet another one of Belmont's friends who wrote about Monsieur.
He reads to her from *Sodom and Gomorrah* where she's called by her
Own name, a maid in Balbec at the Grand Hotel. She speaks there as
She did of Monsieur as a bird, pecking his *croissant and preening
Feathers, deep-eyed mischief, raven hair*. Has she read the passage?


Has she read the book? Did she say that to him, Belmont asks, or did
He make it up? *How much of his book have you been reading in these
Sixty years*? Another test. She wonders if he'll put words in her
Mouth. She's heard he had another name, was in the Occupation busy
In suspicious ways. It's one thing to be friends with Henry Miller and
Another with the Vichy bureaucrats working with Pétain, Pierre Laval.
Belmont carries on about the Sodomites. He'll be, she understands, her
Voice and vehicle, the presence of her past in some dim future.


She says *he'd have his coffee just exactly so. Night turned to day
And day to night. Everything was upside down. Time did not have hours,
Only things to do*. Like him she was a bird but one that sang and
Hopped from branch to branch. She brought the water bottles made
The fire delivered letters for him cleaned the room if he were out and
Picked up all the towels he dropped. *He awoke at four p.m. and wrote
All night, eating almost nothing. He shut out all the sun and burned
The powders that would help him breathe. He disconnected phones.*

III

Her own phone rings. She picks it up. *No, she says, I'm far too busy
And I will be for some time.* But she chats politely for a moment
While Belmont thumbs a copy of *Le Monde* with articles on Watergate,
Although he's thinking about Dreyfus and not Nixon. He's thinking
About loyalty and then he thinks about the very awkward case of
Georges Pelerson. He *is* Georges Pelerson. Celeste hangs up and then
Begins at once where she left off: *Yes, yes the cork lined walls the sealed
Windows fires in summer winter coats. Yes, yes he'd been a Dreyfusard.*

*You know all that. He wouldn't flee the city in the war. He had a special
Kind of courage. I'd go to the basement; he'd go out into the night.* He
Asks her if she still remembers doing Gide, her parody of *Les Nourritures*,
And she says *Oh Nathanaël, I will speak to thee of Monsieur's lady friends.
There is she who made him go out after many years, taxi to the Ritz,
Bell-hops, tips, exhaustion.* And of course Monsieur did go out to the Ritz,
Though not with Gide. Belmont's working nights on *Fear of Flying*;
Suddenly he's got the French for that repeating phrase, *a zippered fuck* . . .

History's a tangle here, but he will sort it all out in the book. No, she says,
*He never lived in Le Cuziat's male brothel; yes I'm sure Agostinelli
Wasn't Albertine. It's true he went out in the night to watch a flagellation
As research. And other ghastly acts. He'd tell me all about them just
As if he'd been to some soirée at Countess Greffulhe's.* All analysis and
Distance, objectivity. *No he didn't drink much alcohol or take those
Drugs you say but just caffeine & powders though he disinfected letters and
Could only look through windows at the hawthorn he had loved.*

IV

Of course she was a prisoner, she knows that. Everyone he knew
Became a prisoner of his book, but there they'll live in time
Beyond their times. Belmont still fears he'll live as Pelerson, who
Swept away his footprints leading to her door. In 1982 Maria Jolas
Will declare that Georges Belmont does not exist, that she and
Joyce and Beckett only knew a Georges Pelerson, collaborationist, who
Calls himself another name & hasn't a remembrance of things past.
In 1982 *Monsieur Proust* will be a German movie called *Céleste*—


Music by Quartet Bartholdy playing César Franck. *No*, she says, *it's
Altogether nonsense that Monsieur set out for that quartet to
Play the Franck carrying a large tureen of soup. He did awake them, one
By one, and brought them back at great expense to play for him. He
Needed one more time to hear the little phrase and all its metamorphoses.*
(Belmont's now forgotten his solution for *a zippered fuck*.) *Monsieur
Once found himself at dinner next to Churchill's table at the time of
Peace talks at Versailles. Then I nearly died of Spanish influenza.*


But the quartet. He asks once more if that was 1916 and, if there was no
Tureen of soup, didn't she provide some fried potatoes and champagne
When they arrived? She says *he wept the day Jaurés was shot; he hated
War but loved his country. Franck and France. They played for him the same
Year as Verdun.* She doesn't ask *Were you a Nazi?* and he rewinds just
A bit and thinks of Krapp in Beckett saying *spool spoooool—box three &
Spool five* and then of Nixon quoted in *Le Monde* maintaining *No erasures
On those tapes.* She thinks about the index in that book he has, her name.

V

*P spends time in conversation with; burns P's notebooks; taking P's
Dictation; pasting manuscripts; parody of Gide; finding spectacles for P* . . .
It's like a tape, a movie. Click & whir and flipping over pages in the
Third biography: *Burns his notebooks & There aren't any gaps!* Krapp is
Saying *Face she had! The eyes!* Georges Belmont is saying *Pelerson*
At some tribunal, disappearing for a decade without civil rights but with
The Henry Millers, *Capricorn* for starters, and a new career that's
Brought him, very busy, to her side. He told her *You must trust me!*

She feels like a theme in César Franck's sonata or a train ride to Cabourg—
A transcribed interview, a Google search before its time. For years they've
Sought her out and she has kept her silence. Alone all night he practiced
Death but also resurrection in the word, *déflagration*. Results 1–10
Of some 1,000 for *Céleste Albaret* (0.11 seconds): Poster, News, & Forum,
See new play at Steppenwolf . . . *an unlettered girl lived a dream. She was
The confidante & maid & mother surrogate* . . . Or was that *Poster-nude,
A fettered girl?* She doesn't say *And you, were you the Jugendfüher?*

She says again *It's time for you to go.* He will not find the sky outside all
Full of Gothas, Zeppelins, or the biwing Valkyries spiraling in spotlit
Crossbeams up. He's coming down from what for seven weeks has kept
Him high. She doesn't say *I loved him* and he doesn't ask *Did he love you?*
She says *Monsieur liked the Abbé Mugnier who used to say Of course
We know that Hell exists, but no one's in it.* She asks *And all these people
Reading Henry Miller or Miss Jong—why not read Monsieur instead?*
He says, *They don't have time.* She smiles . . . And then he's gone . . . .

Through her window spring pollens blow & settle over miles & miles.

# Epilogue: Four Seasons of Vladimir Dukelsky

I—Winter

           ... and the Winter Palace stormed.
Place where khaki tall Kerensky
Felt the fire Scriabin fanned at everything provisional in his *Prometheus*.
He'd huff and puff and blow down what was hardly built.
Crew-cut Angel Gabriel with sex appeal, Dukelsky said of K.
Dukelsky—hot Kiev Conservatory music-man whose own angelic
Sex appeal took the form of Debussy pastiche,
*Aladdine & Palomide* his *Pelléas*.


Would K play Melisande all dressed in skirt and head scarf
Fleeing commissars who paid Dukelsky in potatoes, rice and peas
For a revolutionary hymn à la Glazunov? Newly beggared
Vladimir, obliged to drink a tea he made from bark & carrots,
Wore an avant-garde green coat his mother cut from
Billiard-table baize, shirt and trousers that had been
The winter curtains in his late father's room. He thought he heard
A turbine buzzing somewhere in augmented fourths.


*Modus diaboli!* Cheka spies all whispering in Tristan's
Tritones and diminished fifths. He missed the Maeterlinck Express
From Kiev to Odessa, clicking down the rails chromatically
From C-sharp on to G to conjure fields full of fauns with double flutes.
He took the typhus train, hand & handkerchief to mouth & nose
For more than fifteen days of unrelenting plague.
He hummed the *Marseillaise*: *En-fants*: a fourth. *Pa-trie*, a fourth again.
His mother, *ancien régime*, hid two diamonds up her snatch.

II—Spring

And they escaped. What month was it, Paris? What week in New York?
In Constantinople you could hardly tell. In Odessa they had fled
The rearing horses at the gate, the Red Cavalry, the panic, mobs.
*Navaho* had pushed through ice behind *St. Andrew*, snow and fog
Obscuring Bosphorus for the listing Motherland's ancient ship of refugees.
*Yok, Yok, Effendi* sang the foxtrotting girls; and Tommies drunk on
Turkish beer demanded *Tipperary, K-K-K-Katy*, from the salon trio
At Tokatlian's café. Dukelsky played for silent films most anything he chose.


It was a job. Glazunov for Westerns, Mussorgsky's 'Pictures'
For the Chaplins and some Rimsky-Korsakov for Lang's *Metropolis*.
One night at the Tokatlian he heard a thing he liked. They called it *Swanee*.
The boys in the native band with gusle, oud, and zourna
Made it sound like someone's jihad on the boil, but he heard the
Gershwin somehow coming through. *Yok, Yok, Effendi, it is not beloved
By the authorities but Yanks and Limeys ask for it and 'Hindustan.'*
He memorized it on the spot; it finally felt like spring.


When he reached New York he played the gypsy schmaltz required
For the eateries like Samovar on Second Avenue. He scored
A hooker's favorite songs for fifty cents a piece. His secret life was
Briefly all dodecaphonic when he met the man whose *Swanee* he
Had whistled on the decks of *King Alexander* on his way to an
Ellis Island transit. *Don't fear lowbrow, Kid*, he said; *Tin Pan Alley
Is okay. If you haven't got a melody you ain't American. Heat me up
Some ragtime. We'll change that longhair name to Vernon Duke.*

III—Summer

But he was not yet American, even after he prepared his friend's
*Rhapsody in Blue* for two pianos. His mother sold her diamonds to
An underworld dealer and sent him off to Paris where Diaghilev
Disparaged Duke for vaudeville gigs & rags but commissioned something
Neoclassical and Russian from Dukelsky: *Tutus with Kokoshniks*,
As he said. Enter Flora, lifted high by Zephyrus, dancing *pas de deux*
In an Anacreontic light. The waltz, mazurka, variations & *divertissements
Des muses*: They would even make a corpse dance, said Prokofiev.


Dukelsky still was only twenty-two. The critics liked him. Poulenc
And Stravinsky were impressed, and he got a check for 6,000 francs
And an invitation from Diaghilev to come along to London with the show.
Cocteau, however, slapped him with a glove: *Les Parisiens t'envoyent
De la merde!* But when pressed in earnest for a choice between the swords
And pistols, he sang out: *Embrassons-nous!* Degas had said to Whistler
That he dressed as if he had no talent, Gershwin wrote to D. And D to G:
*I wish my talent didn't sometimes wear a pretty little frilly frock.*


He felt a little less Dukelsky, started feeling Duke. Economies would soon
Be on the rocks, Zephyrus and Flora on the dole. Would there be a
Space to occupy between an Ogden Nash and Mandelstam? He'd set them
Both to music in the end. Certain words he'd dare to write himself:
*Glittering crowds & shimmering clouds in canyons of steel. Jaded roués
And gay divorcées who lunch at the Ritz.* He thought about the autumn
In New York. Why did it seem so inviting? It was 1928 and he took
Another ship. Like Mandelstam in *Epitaph*, he wrapped a rose in furs.

IV—Autumn

Diaghilev soon died, and Gershwin shortly after. Dukelsky grasped at
Balanchine, the movies. Émigré composers headed for L.A. as
Wall Street crashed and Sunset Boulevard survived. Prokofiev heckled him
From Moscow about *maids who become prostitutes to feed their mums*.
His mother ate. He wrote his songs: *April in Paris* on a tuneless upright
In the back of West Side Tony's bistro; *Words Without Music* for
The Ziegfield Follies, 1936. Duke would dig Dukelsky from the rubble
Of Depression. Dancers kicked their can-cans on the silver screen.


But did Dukelsky dig the tunes of Duke? Count Basie would in time,
Sinatra would—and, born on his own birthday, even Thelonius Monk.
*Can you play again*, Sam Goldwyn asked him laughing, *that dyspeptic chord?*
Musicologists have praised the two adjacencies preceding an initial E,
The lower raised chromatically to match the half step in a symmetry:
*A-pril in Par-is*. Meanwhile, Mandelstam still lived, weeping for
The wooden Russia of his youth. *Gradually the servants sort out piles
Of overcoats. They wrap a rose in furs*. In Cyrillic and for choir, an epitaph.


For whom? Diaghilev? Dukelsky? Mandelstam? Academic serialism
Shut down tonal elegists and Tin Pan Alley crooners came to terms
With Elvis after yet another World War. Who remembered the bucolic
*Zephyrus*, phantasmagoric *Epitaph* for choir? Alexander Feodorovich
Kerensky hummed a phrase stuck in his head from something that he couldn't
Name and walked the Stanford campus in the twilight to his little office
Where he wrote a book about the revolution no one read. He wrapped
A rose in furs & it was autumn: in Leningrad & Paris, Palo Alto & New York.

# Part Three

## The HIJ and Other Poems

I

# Early Evening Walk, Suffolk, Christmas 1973

Hacheston: the village still a village
And inhabited by villagers.
Low fog. A brisk wind off the sea.

No one out but Mrs. Deben pushing
On her baby carriage all full of wood.
I knew what she would say:

*Have you seen my little baby, pray?*
Oh not today. Oh not today.
My daughters, three and five,

Were safe inside their mother's
Childhood home. Gray smoke from
The chimney curled into the sky.

Through a window of the last house
Along the street called The Street
I saw an old woman cutting up the veg

And dropping carrots, onions, greens
Into a pot. In the next room, just
Behind, an even older man played

The violin. He stopped, looked out at me
As I looked in, waved his bow,
And started up again.

I turned my collar up
And walked into the wind.
I was as happy as I've ever been.

# Fragment: At the Tomb of Henry Howard

*Last of the East Anglian Poems, left unfinished, April, 1995*

    . . . there
By the north wall of the chancel,
Church of Saint Michael,
Framlingham. He was ambitious, yes,
In matters touching armorial bearings,
But useful, too, at Landrecy, Bolougne.
There was no treason in his heart.
For a while he served the king
Who sent him to the block.

A proud and foolish boy, they said.
His effigy's so still.
Jane and Katherine, daughters, at his head.
At his feet, Thomas and Northampton.
His wife beside him, still.
So austere and prayerful are they all
You'd never guess this rigid father was the boy
Who broke out windows of the London burgesses
And stepped from prison in the fleet
To legend in the gallery at Arundel
And Thomas Nashe's prose

    . . . there
By the north wall of the chancel.
And in his line—strict iambic genealogies
That parse a Howard or Aeneas.
Again, I've come to pay respects.
I've sought him here before.

That a shield's quarterings
Should spell the end of such a man!
Had he, as in Nash, born heraldry
Of love before ambition—*militat omnis amans*
And a knotted sword—then all were well.
But he carried into battle on a quarter of his shield
Sign of him who'd be an heir-apparent,

Edward the confessor's arms.
Was it a jest (although his Mabry blood
Conferred the right)?
No one laughed before the scaffold that he mounted
In a January rain of the next year.


They brought him here eventually . . .
                                      There
By the north wall of the chancel
Where, if he were not a soldier but a saint,
I'd pray to him, I think,
As spirit of the place and emblem
Of a loss

# Artemis, Aging . . .

(For Diana, on her 65<sup>th</sup> birthday)

But of course she does not age! Immortal, she
Does what she has always done: There is no future tense
To drag her down, to soften her hard body,
Compromise her chastity. Through the ages she is
What she always is: There is no past except for those
She touches, touched, will touch: They rise and fall
With time, but she is timeless. Does she envy them
Their human grace to change? Callisto, found with child,
Became a constellation with her son, Arktos, rising up
Behind her in the circumpolar sky. Actaeon turned
Into a stag. I've seen Diana at her bath but never was
Devoured by my hounds, only by my longing.
Young, she moved like the wife of Menelaos in the
Eyes of Telemachus—*straight as a shaft of gold*.
But even Helen by that time had changed: Housefrau
In the great Lacedaemon mansion house, she began
To age. The red-haired king found his lady all the more
Amazing and the struggle on the beachhead year by year
Receded in his memory. Vindictive Artemis forgets
Nothing and does not forgive. Her eternal present
Is as sterile as the moon's. If she could change, she
Might be like the woman called by her Roman name
Reading in a book beside the fire in my own house.
She has come down all these years with me, and she
Is getting old. She turns the pages slowly, then looks up.
Her wise ironic glance is *straight as a shaft of gold*.

II

# The Double: after Heine

The night is still, sleeping in the streets,
And still the house in which my lover lived.
She is sleeping somewhere else and yet
Her house in this same place stands still.
Time stands still. Still as well the man who stands
And stares into her window—someone else,
But also me. In the moonlight, me—
But also someone else: Doppelgänger
Made of me and wringing hands, who shakes
With grief and rage, dark and doublegoer,
Pale companion, mon semblable, frère,
Who makes my Liebesleid his own, takes
The night that's mine, takes in stillness now
My lover and my witness and my love.

# After George Seferis

1. Euripides the Poet

Euripides the poet
Growing old between the holocaust at Troy
And the Reichstag fire
Beheld the sea and heard the oceanic laughter
Of the gods. He liked the sea-shore caves
Where he could be alone
And try to see the net of human veins, designed
To capture us like animals, as something
To be torn and broken through.
He was a bitter, friendless man. When he died,
He died not in Athens but in Macedon
Where dogs ate his flesh and dragged his bones
Around and around the city walls.

2. Isaac and Iphigenia

And Isaac said: This is my body, my flesh.
To Iphigenia, whose father was not
Halted in his work by any intervening hand,
I offer it in marriage, though I am but a boy
And she a virgin bleeding from her throat.
She will take me to her, she will fondle me. I will
Be entirely hers. Our fathers should have met.
Imagine Agamemnon saying "Abraham!"
And Abraham responding "Agamemnon!" Imagine
Poets asking them: Who is to be saved,
Who is to be sacrificed? Our dear son will know.
Our dear daughter will reveal it. But first we will praise
The Many and the One, the Lord
And the lords, the Father and our fathers,
And all the calculating gods and God.

3. Iphigenia and Isaac

And Iphigenia said: This is not my body, my flesh.
From Isaac, whose father *was* interrupted
In his work by an intervening hand, I withhold *I am*.
They told me I had come to an altar for Achilles
And I found another child like me. I wept to behold him.
Agamemnon never held out hands to Abraham.
Our fathers never met. No one knows or *will* know who
Is led to sacrifice and who is saved before the hour.
I was the hour. Only we are daughter and the son.
I think we are spirits lingering beyond our time, for
They have truly murdered me. Troy and The Temple fell.
Let poets curse the many and the One, the Lord
And the lords, the Father and our fathers,
And all the calculating gods, and God.

# Other Lives

> *The life I could have lived, the better one*
> *Is also mine. Who else can claim it?*
>     Ernest Sandeen

And the one that is worse? That one too—
Or the plural, those lives neither better
Nor worse but only unimaginably different.
Think of those months I loved that girl

Whose name I can't remember; it was fifty
Years ago. And the other two whose movement
Out of darkness into light I did not foresee.
Had I not three times said to one when some-

One other came, forgive me but I cannot
Not do this thing that I'm about to do,
It would have been more singular, more sanguinary.
Not done and nothing left of me but you.

# After Horace

Dear Old Pal from Columbus, Ohio—
I'm sorry to hear you became a judge
Like my father. I'm well out of all that.
I didn't like his kind of life at all

Or that of his cronies. Until the class reunion
I hadn't a clue you were even a lawyer.
Tempus fugit, etcetera. As for me, my days
As a Prof at the College are over.

Now I can write or just hang out in the town.
In the Forum, I like to watch the girls hustling
To lunch from the wide office block door,
Wobbling on their heels, twitching their asses.

Those who stay at their desks are helping their
Billionaire boss cooking all his books,
Telling our fortune, fucking him on an aileron chair.
The usurer and the satyr are one. When the sun

Gets hot, I head for the bath. I wash the dust
Of the Circus Maximus from my face
And my eyes and my hair. I dangle my feet
In the water, ease the cramp in my arch.

Unlike you and my father, I don't have to
Care if someone important's nearby.
The hell with him, and what he might think
Of my paunch. If I go to Cincinnati tomorrow,

I can go cheap on a mule—no five slaves need
To follow me down the Interstate road
With a cask of wine and a portable loo. The best
Of it is, I don't have to make up my mind.

I can go tomorrow or not. Maybe I'll just stay home
And read Mark Twain, watch the guys playing ball.
I haven't anything pressing, and I've lost my ambition,
Even though my father, like you, was a judge.

*Horace, from Satires I, 6*

# Kolonos Hippios

The old men who scrambled out at last from behind
      some rocks and trees below Poseidon's great Horse Hill
That they called *kolonos hippios* and was famous for the rider
      whose immortal name these coloni still bore and was
Still guarded by Eumenides of black night and bright day

Had a kind of tabloid curiosity and mean prurient desire
      to hear the very worst. Make the blind man tell us everything
They said as one—for of course they were a chorus—make him
      spill his guts about his mother-fucking patricidal brother-sister
Fathering accomplished from the very womb that bore him.

Make him tell us how the goo of his eyes smelled like vile jelly
      running from the brooch he used to gouge them on his thumbs
And palms, and make him tell us why his swollen pierced ankles
      never healed once the king he'd murder one day (& he's done it now)
Left him on a hillside outside Thebes and what it's like to stumble

As an exile place to place and why he wishes he were never born.
      Sophocles himself was born at K.H.—the Horse Hill Rider's
Riding place—& not Agora Hill (*kolonos agorias*) in Athens proper
      out of which came Theseus to chastise the old men in the chorus
And at last to organize the rescue of Antigone (there beside

Her father!) who'd be briefly caught and kidnapped soon
      by Creon and a group of louts. Tell us all the dirt on Oedipus
Shouted the old men; we'll put it in our paper, put it on T.V.
      Easy, Geezers, warned the noble Theseus; we can have you all
Arrested well before your *kommos*—that's your dialogue that's coming

With the Tragic Hero in a meter that I never learned to scan
      in school. Anyway, you'll all end up as Roman property and bound
To the soil that you think you're so in love with by about AD 300
      or in a 1950s working-class ghetto high-rise served by Hellenic
Railways, which will never whisk *you* out of there, and accessible

From Avenue Konstantinopoulos just in case some literary scholar
        might come visit. Let me know then how it feels.
It may feel better not to have been born, but I anticipate a bit like
        Old Tiresias. Try us at our web site: Cityfathers@Athens.org
That's an oracle you might well consult from time to time.

It will tell you that your sacred grove is a polluted slum where
        nightingales don't sing, there's no laurel blossoming, no olives offered
By Athena to the riders of Poseidon's horses flashing eyes and sparking
        hoofs off paving stone. But never mind. Your editor himself insists
That the author of your most famous version lies buried somewhere

Like the hero of your play will be if we continue this in order to be
        venerated like the head of Brân the Blessed under London's tower
For frustration of all enemies and to keep inviolate the land
        not because he wrote you into this upcoming grim exchange with
Poor Rex without a kingdom who would die to bring you life

With good peace right after a convincing victory in bad times
        but because he hosted once a doctor called Asclepius, gave him just
Exactly what you can't or won't provide—the wine & olives, lamb & peppers,
        fresh fruit and (why not) a pretty girl, or (why not) a boy.
Anyway, Asclepius fucked the girl or boy or both and drank the wine

And ate the olives and the lamb, the peppers and the fresh fruit
        and ended up Director of the most corrupt insurance scam in Athens,
Old geezers treated for the same thing—impotence—no matter what was
        wrong with them and any sweet young thing appearing in the ER
Complaining of desire sent upstairs at once to see the CEO.

But on with it. He's still got Polynices yet to deal with, and Creon too.
        Do the *kommos* and return the whole proceedings to your sponsor:
Everybody wants a piece of him, his body for a blessing in whatever earth.
        And yet he'll seem according to the Messenger's last speech more
Like mist evaporating off the sea in sunlight: Kind of up and disappeared,

He'll say. He like I mean seemed to vanish then and there while thundered
    Zeus and howled Antigone a lot and beat her breasts and wailed like
And walked around in circles saying sorry Oh she'd lost it to photographers,
    and he himself just *nothing* of a sudden just a nothing suddenly and he was
*Gone* man and nowhere when he'd just before been right there and then.

But before that magic, this: The dreaded *kommos* and the who who who
    are you before the owl of Athena on its bough and I am Oedipus and
*Aoiiiii* please the gods not him and yes the final ordure of all outrage
    swellfoot father of my sister I am him you loathe and who men have
Called pierceankle angle-prized and angel-priced I will be but what you

Make of it when nobody looks for me and nobody asks my poisoned name.

# Biblical Archaeology

(Re: The recent discovery of *situlae* at Gath,
destructive level 9th Century B.C.E.)

. . . for there were indeed these *'opalim*
That so afflicted Philistines in First *Samuel* 6
That they returned the Ark with golden
Models of them as a placatory gift . . .

King James' committee has it *emerods*—
*Emerods in their secret parts*. But golden
Models of them? Of their hemorrhoids?
The trespass offering included also golden mice.

*Ye shall make images of your emerods*
*And ye shall give glory unto the God of Israel*
And with any luck your secret parts
Won't require more than a mild steroid cream.

In Hebrew Sabbath recitations *'opalim*
is not pronounced aloud. It's root's
A root, a rise, a swelling upward, like
The votive phalluses of Gath, gift *situlae*

Uncircumcised and only half erect. O impotence!
O Philistines who sent back the images
Full of milk or even semen, god Min a gold
Priapic figure on each one. O dire affliction!

They had ED and not the *emerods*. They called
Out abjectly to the God of Israel: take
These golden mice and golden *'opalim*.
A cat for every man's restored virility.

Day and night our famous goldsmiths work.
Some day archaeologists will know it isn't
Piles at issue but our progeny when unspoken *'opalim*
Still glows in *Samuel* like a rune.

Our women weep and howl at the moon.

# Lorenzo England Clan Alvis Lupu XLV

With Nottingham asleep in him, he walked in
The Etruscan places, wrote his last book,

Sought to build a ship of death constructed
Well enough to sail in the underworld. Frieda

And Maria nursed him as he coughed blood
And tried once more to breathe. That was in *Ad Astra*

At Vence. Maria was Maria Huxley
not Maria Magdalene or Mary Mother of God

For Christsake! He'd gods enough to spare
A few for those that Virgil knew.

Feminists abhor him now, though he was
Strangely feminine himself—&

Etruscans? We don't know how they spoke
But *L alvis lupu XLV*. On a wall in Tarquinia he loved

The boy with the double flute: He would have
Played his music if he'd had the breath.

Would that have scattered the Apocalyptic beasts?
Would it *Filius Meus*?

It's a kind of drowning, dying of TB.
His Jesus Christ was no

Etruscan boy, but adult living member
Of dismembered Osirus, not

As we had thought, swallowed by the crab
Of the Nile, but by Our Lady of Isis. Oh the priestess

Cradled him with pity and with pride.
He completed her remembering.

His memory was in her helping hands alone,
Her magnanimity, her mouth.

# Modernato Pizzicato

*O Lynx keep watch on my fire* he had written in Pisa
and *Dryad* he'd called her a long time back
and she thought the *new subtlety of eyes* was probably hers
*dove sta memoria* when she read it in the his prison poems
in her Küssnacht sanatorium . . .

        *E.P. loves H.D.*— it could
have been encircled with a heart, carved by a couple of kids
on a tree. From the wreckage of Europe they groped their way
toward what they remembered and loved.
And at Küssnacht that clinic was fine for filming
a bust: Dick and Nicole at Dr. Brunner's healing-place,
*Scott loves Zelda* carved by actors on the widest conifer.
Pound had put a eucalyptus seed in his coat when
the Partisans marched him away from hills above Rapallo.
It had the face of a cat: *O Lynx keep watch on my fire.*
And she was herself a feline, an eidolon Helen to boot.
As Freud's analysand she watched the local extras in halls,
a rich girl taking the talking cure talking and talking. Change
the movie to *Borderline* and she is the star, a demi-monde
neurotic with her dipsomaniac beau. Who knows why
they're here? Or Jason Robards and Jennifer Jones who
drive each other's Dick & Nic around town; Jill St. John
is no *San Juan with a belly ache writing ad posternos*,
but she squeaks like a ditsy mouse and shows her pointy tits.

What all fits this case? A pretty face, of course,
a march to the line, a dance to the rhythm, the time.
Rhyme it with mime and bring in the rest of the cast:
Tom and Viv, Gertrude and Alice, Nora and Jim—
Billyam Williams and Freytag-Loringhaven the mad.
*Ulysses loves Penelope* they carve on yet another tree.
Helen's at the door of Dr. Brunner; Paris is a patent fiction
she complains. Let's to Lake Geneva for a sail. P. Pudovkin
writes in *Close-up*, Bryer's cinema mag, regarding the art
of the cut, but who has the knife any more or the nail?

It's closing time at the jail, the privileged asylum,
contagious hospital, letterpress printer's, the ruined town.
Close up the closet of cut-up text & cut out hearts & heroes
cut down to size. Some guy on TV is singing pizzicato lies.
Someone's baby sits right down and cries.

# Their Flims

                  films, that is. A typo just as easy
an *essai* as William Faulkner's standing
on the set with Howard Hawkes
charged with coming up with something quick to
spice the dialogue in Hem his rival's
*Have or Have Not*, moved from Florida and Cuba
all the way to Martinique, Hawkes saying
*Well well well well  <u>try</u> something
here*. And the novelist's response: *Was you
ever bitten by a dead bee*? All for Walter Brennen,
Bogart and Becall gone off already for
a drink with Scott who'd not have bothered with the big
film of 1939 (because by then *The Last
Tycoon* was on the fire) if he hadn't had a contract still
to honor even if he was fifteenth and not the first
to have a go at Miss Leigh's Miss Scarlett.

Their films. Their fame consists of something else,
a flame and flame-out, both. How to have
both haven for a talent in your palm and payment
in your fist to gobsmack anyone who'd
make you write in anagrams derived from text by
Margaret Mitchell? Not a bloody word
you haven't picked with tiny forceps out of Tara's
Torah, mate: When you're bitten by
a dead bee you'll know the nature of a sting-
ing cut, an improvisation by the broad: *You know
how to whistle, don't you*? What's the difference
between Vichy cops and Southern gents
or officers in Rebel uniforms wrapped
like mummies in the Stars and Bars? Bogy's luck
with Miss Becall and Gable's reassurances
that he was never gay didn't trouble pages adding up
in *Absalom* or point of view adjusted in
the fictive life of Irving Thalburg, movie mogul, when
the daughter saying I, I, I has got beyond her depth

and can't produce *Producer's Daughter* as a
college girl at Bennington. What added up was
adding up: the debts. To whom however ask the question:
*Now I owe you one?* The actress on her knees
in some lost outtake in the pre-coded days in Hollywood
saying *Bet you don't believe I ever read your book?*

# Family Apocrypha
*A Slashed Painting by John Singer Sargent*

The large Sargent painting, subsequently slashed,
Of my distant cousin Hoffman, Alice Green,
Was photographed in Paris by Michelle's Studio
In 1909. Alice had complained of standing still

For hours at what Sargent called a "sitting," and
That she was forced to bring, day after day,
The fresh roses herself. But *he* was who he was.
This would be a "Sargent," after all, and grand

As it could be, grand as his pictures of the other
Ladies in her circle captured by the genius
Of his hand. *Dab dab dab* she heard, and *Stand still
Will you please Miss Green*, and *Mind the rose.*

She minded roses, was in fact allergic, just like
Monsieur Proust, and she had to dab dab dab
At her running nose with a little handkerchief she
Brought from her hotel. Three of them, in fact.

He asked her to open up the book he had brought her,
Place it on the table with the roses, read a poem.
Oh it was John Keats! *Now look up*! he said,
*And gaze at the lawn through the magic casement*

*At a thing fled forever from its image in the poem.
It's lost*, he said, *but you—I'll save you for the ages
If you just stand still another hour, another month.
Tell me once again who this Hoffman is.*

She wondered if she really knew. She would marry him
Of course, but she doubted that she loved him.
What did it matter, he was wealthier than she. He was
A (white) descendent of George Washington, and

He was paying for this portrait as a wedding gift.
Hoffman, that is, and not the father of her country—
If indeed it *was* her country any more, if indeed
He were the father of it. Hoffman had her reading

Aaron Burr and other members of the Founding Fops,
As he liked to say, telling her she'd make a better
Picture even than the *Portrait of Madame Pierre Gautreau*.
*I am a Washington*, he said, *but only on the side*.

She didn't know the oldest of old tales—*A man of means,*
*My dear, and mean enough to many when he'd*
*Met them with the line he'd taken from the artist's*
*Great new friend: You are a woman out of Henry James!*

That had taken them exactly to this point and not beyond.
She stood. The artist dab dab dabbed. As yet she didn't know
That Hoffman was an outrageous rake who stalked
The beautiful and famous through salons and country houses

And the continental spas. Standing tall and straight as
Archer's arrow held in Eros' hand, she didn't know
He'd tell her *all* when every honest hour ticked beyond
The help of any art. Would he rip the white bodice

From her even whiter breasts while she, before she
Slashed the canvas worth a Whistler or Degas,
Looked into his smirking face and said *My raffish*
*Mr. Crass: I leave an image only of an image.*

*Take it for a song— a kind of testament, a trespass.*

# The Baronesses

It's a pity that William Carlos Williams couldn't have met
The Baroness friend of Thelonious Monk instead of
His own Baroness Elsa von Freytag-Loringhoven. No doubt
About it, Baroness Pannonica de Koenigswarter would have
Been a better bet. Although she dug jazz rather then poetry,
Williams would surely have warmed her heart with
His poems about pure products of America, metric figures,
The gold 5 on a fire-truck, lonely streets. He could have
Read them to her in that room with the terrific outlook over
The Hudson where a baby grand and a night of coffee and
Good conversation were always ready for Monk & his friends.
But alas he instead had for his long-suffering self
The unwanted attentions of Elsa von Freytag-Loringhoven, a
Baroness Thelonious Monk might have liked. She was
No rich patron, exactly—in fact not at all. Down and out as a
Pure product of America, she might have cadged a drink from
The Baroness Pannonica de Koenigswarter, or just a dime.
Or she might have asked to spend the night in her home
In the Stanhope hotel. Lots of people did—and listened to
Records of Horace Silver's "Nica's Dream," Gigi Gryce's
"Nica's Tempo," Kenny Dorham's "Tonica," and of course
The tune by Thelonious Monk, all composed for the former
K.A.P.(for Pannonica) Rothschild who married the pilot
And banker Jules de Koenigswarter, later a French diplomat.
But in fact they never met, mostly because the poor and crazy
Baroness Elsa von Freytag-Loringhoven died in the gas that
She or her lover allowed to escape in her dingy Dada digs
In Rue Barrault on 14 December of 1927, a year when the
Barroness Pannonica de Koenigswarter was still only a girl
Of twelve out in the fields with her gifted father Nathaniel
Charles Rothschild hunting bugs for his entomological pastime
Which etymologically led, said Monk, to her name: Pan-
Nonica of Eastern Europe's Pannonian plain, a butterfly her
Father had found and liked. As for Elsa von Freytag-Loringhoven,
She was hot not for Monk—who after all was only six at the time—
But for William Williams, doctor and poet, thirty-eight in 1921.

She wore a coal-scuttle as a hat, tin cans on her breasts, and
Exhibited with Man Ray and Duchamp in circa those days
A plumbing-pipe she called "God." Williams followed her
Home from the show where she offered to give him
The very thing that he, as a doctor, treated for free in half
His artist friends in New York—a case of the clap.
He withdrew, but she followed. All the way to Williams' house
In New Jersey. At that point everything's right out of
Somebody's travesty of Restoration excess on a Provincetown
Stage: she arrives, he runs, she pursues, he calls for help from
His wife, she curses in German, he shoves her away, she punches
His face, he punches her face, she hides in a tree, he shakes on
Her branch, she falls and stumbling recovers, his wife throws a
Rolling pin in the air, she laughs, he cries, she disappears in the night
With police in hot pursuit and Mrs. W.W. singing out something
A bit like "Well, you needn't" or "By-ya," "Off minor,"
Or "Nutty"—all tunes by Thelonious Monk. Round about midnight
Monk would arrive at Baroness Pannonica's place. There he would
Play the piano for hours, for days. Mostly he didn't talk.
Sometimes he sat and stared at the keys. In the end the Baroness
Took on the jobs that Monk's exhausted wife no longer performed.
She got him to eat, got him to take his pills, got him now and then
Out of the house to perform. She must have loved the man.
He fell at last into a silence deep as Ezra Pound's in Venice.
He no longer played. She let him behave as he liked, dressing up
In his natty way in the morning but lying all day in bed in his
Crisp clean shirt with a coat and tie. That went on for three years.
If Baroness Elsa von Freytag-Loringhoven and William Williams
Had come for a visit or house-call, they would have learned
A thing or two about the pure products of America and respect
Verging on awe. It would have been quiet there as the grave
And tending to the sublime. With Baronesses keeping watch on
Either side of the bed, the doctor poet might have picked the
wet hair from the pianist's eyes and watched him with compassion.

# Asheville Out

*i.m. Charles Olson and Thomas Wolfe*

                so you've only a museum now
and not a college at all
although I understand the buildings still exist near the town
where religion has reclaimed the real estate that
John Rice took for the muses after he scandaled at Rollins
lecturing on the classics in his jock. *What . . . ?* she says—
but she's in Asheville here at the *Mountain Museum*
with Annie Albers and Ruth Asawa and M.C. Richards
*Women of the College* up on walls
their paintings and prints and stills from documentary films
works and days from the place
where poets, if not painters, were so macho they hadn't the time
to read, for example, Hilda Morley's delicate poems.
*Who. . .?* she says, young and pretty docent, and I think
of docile women among genital toughs out there
but also of dear Hilda when I met her, Yaddo in the 70s, when
still she was unpublished, getting really old, still telling
all those stories about Stefan Wolpe's Parkinson's –
little paper-wads of poems slipped under my door at night,
her Dickinsonian habit of abasement followed by abrupt display
of weirdly-offered & prodigious genius—
Wolpe her great lover and her husband and the reason why
she didn't publish for so long.
I think the most erotic photograph I've ever seen
was of Hilda once in *Ironwood* where the young and lovely girl
bites into an apple smiling with her eyes at Wolpe
middle-aged and briefly eminent composer
while he grins longing back at her on the Lee Hall front porch
and the grand love between them
positively shimmers in the air, in the lake behind them,
in the green mountains above—

                and Tom Wolfe only
wanted out
of all this, the hills, the little town, the boarding house
managed by his mum: *Just off the car line;*

*Large Lawns, Reasonable Rates, Newly furnished Throughout.*
*Our Auto Rides You from the Station for Free*
*No Sick Folks Here.* Did I know, she asks,
any of the really *famous* poets? Dorn, yes; Creeley, yes;
Robert Duncan, yes & for a while & in a way.
'Twas as if I said I'd seen Shelley plain.
Days of *Idaho Out.*
Days of *Gloucester Out.* Asheville out beyond and
south I used to drive on family holidays
my father stuck it in reverse on mountain curves because
our Plymouth—1948—couldn't manage the climb
except by backing up. Scott Fitzgerald didn't meet Tom Wolfe
in 1936 because the six-foot-seven native was
in Germany for the Olympics in a U.S. diplomatic box just west
of Hitler on the day that Owens won his first gold.
He exploded in a raucous Rebel cheer that drew the Führer's ire:
*Who's the big oaf with their ambassador?*
And who's the man in Asheville with the crazy wife
whose books were all the rage before the crash and all
the unemployed, for who cared in 1936 about those flappers
in East Egg or was it West those rich idlers on the Riviera?
*I don't know*, she says, *but . . .*
nor did the two giants ever meet—had you
asked Wolfe to climb on Olson's shoulders they'd have
been together something getting onto fourteen feet tall
and a useful human ladder for a second-story man breaking
into Biltmore place. But what's the first story
and she says *Did you teach out there yourself?* Of course
Maximus & Eugene Gant never walked along the Blue Ridge Highway
but they might have done it just as my father
might have gotten round that turn and backed the car
to Cherokee where nothing much is going on
beyond the poverty, casino gambling, Indians playing Indians
for some snotty gringo's snotty children now. But then
there was the first story. It's about three bears.
Alas it's true that some men forgot their obligations and

their clan's rites and found themselves with long hair on their bodies
and without their thumbs
and on their hands and knees, the kinsmen still of Hanging Maw
and Double Head and even John Ridge
they assumed names like Jackson Johnson Jefferson
and knew they must be hunted as they hid
until they had to hunt themselves. What kind of creatures
walk together on the road from Asheland out
of caves and down from trees and into talking leaves
inscribed in signs for eighty-six sounds
borrowed by Sequoia from the Greek and Roman and Cyrillic?
*What*? She says. Days of *Gloucester Out*, I say.
*Days of what*? she says. Those, I say, were the days.

III

# Nightmare Quatrains

I—Fragment

I dreamed he was beating my daughter.
And when he had struck her
Several times on the head and in the face
She stared at me, amazed.

Her right eye was gone. In its place
Was a kind of transparent film
Through which I could see directly
Into her brain.

II—Mon Semblable

I was still maybe under forty when that old man
—Emeritus, I guessed, still with an office
And his books—turned back in the hall having peed
Down his left leg before he reached the loo.

He walked toward me sans shame, sans shuffling
Right side first, or turning to the wall.
He walked with my lost daughter, stern eyes
Upon me saying *you two, you too* . . .

# Shostakovich Quartet #15, op. 144
# Rehearsing the Beethoven String Quartet, May 1974

*(five movements all marked Adagio)*


No no, he said in rehearsal,
Dying and thinking that this was the last
Music he'd write      No

He said      it's not slow enough
Play it slower than slow
(The four of them slowly nodding their heads)

Adagio of the grave adagio of the cremation glow
Slower than slow    So    slow
That the audience tiptoes creeping out of the hall

And all the flies drop dead in the air

# Parting at a College Parking Lot

The last time we met was in a parking lot
Beside the post office. He was sending out a stack
Of cards announcing a change of address.
I'd not seen him for a long time and understood
There had been a scandal of some kind, hushed
Up because he was a priest. He couldn't meet
My eye and clearly didn't know if I were privy
To events in his past that had flared again into
His life and brought him down, or not.
He had done me kindnesses and I admired
As much as I could understand of work
He'd done that made him famous. I said
I'd miss him. He said he'd spent the last
Three days doing things that old men do
And that today he'd burned his letters—some
From men like Bohr and Einstein. He said
He'd miss me too. When I came here, his name
Was on everybody's lips, his work a legend.
He was now about to creep out of town in
The night. He went back to Ireland and he died.

# A Winter Night

My friend's son comes by our house
In the night. He's not expected. He's had
Some difficult times and he's hurting and
His family is far away in Cagnes-sur-Mer.

I listen. I tell my old man's tales—I too
Experienced that; time will make it better.
We don't know each other well. Winter's
Long in this Midwestern town.

Winter's long and he's been walking through
The darkened neighborhood at night.
Up late, we were reading books and listening
To Haydn string quartets. We closed the books,

Turned the music off. He says he feels just like
Dostoevsky's Idiot. He also feels French, like
His mother, Swedish like his father. He's been
Alone in the American Midwestern night.

I think of several ways to say that time will
Make it better. No, it really won't, he says.
My wife smiles sympathetically, gives him a
Hug at the door. I've insisted that I drive him

Back to student digs nearby. The neighborhood's
Not really safe. When we get there, we talk
Some more in the car, shake hands, and then he
Goes inside. I wait to see a light come on.

Suddenly I realize my hand is dripping blood.
In the garden of Asclepius all who took the
Temple cure left their wound-dressings on the
Branches of a sacred tree. The old know that

Time will heal all wounds. The young know
That time is a walk through a Midwestern winter
Night, where every icy limb is hung with
Fetid bandages and every single tree has died.

## Vanity of Human Wishes

*. . . long day in the sun at Half Moon Bay, way-back
table by the Workshop door, long night
in the town. Coltrane, Davis, Evans . . . dawn*

                        Stanford and San Francisco, 1964

Round about mid-year we found our decade
drifting on toward myth and
half got it, half got lost in decades not our own—
dizzy flappers, strikers on the dole.
Named for Lenin—"I go by my initials, I'm V.I."—
you really were our Byron, biking out of early
Thom Gunn poems like *On the Move,*
*The Unsettled Motorcyclist's Vision of his Death.*

You tried but didn't manage to die young.
Who could ever have foreseen
how death would come for you in middle age—the first
heart attack among us,
not some T.E. Lawrence wipe-out on the road—
your daughter walking out to get the mail and
coming back to find you on the sofa,
still holding on your dead lap a live cat that
strayed into the clapboard house with
a bit of land you called the Hot Rocks Ranch
inland from the edge of the Pacific.

When I remember the day we met, met for sure
in yet another time, when Augustan habits
weren't for owning up, it isn't
all the tales you told I think of first—
how you'd written Everly Brothers songs, played professional
ball, knew the actresses in Hollywood—but that you
instinctively called me Johnny, something
no one had done since I was ten. Johnny, you said,
we did the Juvenal he cribbed this from in
High School Latin class when I ran
with a West Side gang. I'm still a communist.

I still do drugs. What am I doing in 18th century England?
What the hell kind of hopeless geezer
am I turning into out here on the coast when a Brit
with dropsy and a wig who calls his thing an imitation
makes me think I'm reading my obit.

# A Reunion

At his fiftieth class reunion, he spent a long time
Talking to the old woman he was in love with
When they were both seventeen. She was never
In love with him. He used to stare at her in class
When she was bent over her work in deep concentration.
And at night, yes, he did with his body what boys do
With her imagined body as his eidolon. When he arrived
At the reunion, she greeted him with a warm embrace.
In her view they had always been friends, "dear friends."
He could feel her small breasts on his chest the way
He used to when he'd sometimes get to dance with her
At school parties before she'd leave early to make out
In a parked car with the person she was taking seriously
At the time and eventually married. They talked
About what two ageing people talk about: their illnesses
And doctors, their grandchildren, missing the dead.
What if he'd told her what he was remembering then?
That he used to pay her little brother a dollar if he
Promised to mention his name over the family dinner?
What if he'd told her how fervently he'd often prayed
That she loved him, and, when it was finally clear
That she didn't, how he'd stopped believing in love?

# Falcon on the Alley Wall

First light of morning and a large shape
Dips beneath above   around   a crisscross
Of the city wires, brings its breakfast
To our alley wall. He's eight or ten feet
From the window just behind my desk and seems
Much less than that once my face is pressed
Against the pane. He sees me there.
He holds the rodent under his great claw
And fluffs the bright down on his breast just
Catching the dawn. He looks at me.
I look at him. His meal squirming in his fist.

A postman and a boy on a bike and two
Chattering schoolgirls walk beneath his perch
And do not notice him up there at all.
He turns his head and watches closely
As they round the corner by the cans of trash,
Get on with the getting on of things.
As for me I want to see this sighting right.
By the time I've run to get the bird book thumbing
*Falco peregrinus, Falco rusticolus, kle kle kle*
*We'shew we'shew at eyrie, kek kek kek*
And so on          he has gone

# Demographics: Evening News

Begin with Flowmax, guys, and maybe you can
Get through famine, earth quake, plague
Without a bad surprise, urgency once more an
Intervention, stream constricted by a swollen gland.

Ladies, watch those bones: if you forget your
Fosamax plus D, you'll look like a hula hoop at
Neighbor niece's happy birthday fête—so
Bent down, you won't know any more what's up.

Do you remember Camron Swayze, Huntley-Brinkley,
Cornkite? You'll need those laxatives and
Denture glue on offer here between the drought
In Africa and Asian floods. If the latest genocide

Makes you depressed, there's Zoloft, Prozac.
Heart is in your mouth? It's no doubt acid reflux.
So ask your Doc about *the healing purple pill*.
If all that *pro* or *loft* or *max* is making you feel

Ill, try a bit of antidote: *dip* or *con* or *min*:
*Dipsominacon* if you're maxed out, proleptic,
Lofted off your hemorrhoids like a laser guided
missile damaging collateral that bombed

In your account like Borax in your bowels.
Smoke from all those wars killed Edward Murrow.
Where there's smack there's fire. If there's crack
They're hiring. You were young and thought

You'd change the world once upon. Now you
Merely fear the worst has not been done.
Our punch line's from Viagra:
Dig it, ancients, for *The best are yet to come.*

# When They Sent Him Back

*(On hearing that the site of St. Elizabeths mental hospital, where Ezra Pound spent 13 years in captivity, is to become a new Center of Electronic Surveillance)*

When they sent him back to Italy.
When they kept the poet's brain at Saint Elizabeths.
When they knew they'd find a method to decode
Occult and paranoid connections among
Disparate data. More occult and more disparate,
More coded Zeus amen, than any Io mother load in
Any other brain they had. A time and a method.
When they waited there and thought.
When they incubated. When they loved and hated.
Incubated and debated. Waited with a baited breath.
When they anagrammed it A.B Nepir. Obtained
From E.P. Brain their Chief of Staff for New Empire
Poetry: *Really Is About the Bombs*. The bombs away.
To keep at bay with baited breath and method.

That explains his total silence in his final years.
The distress among his friends and peers.
When they kept his brain at Saint Elizabeths.
The accumulations and connections. All the data.
All the deuteronomy. The great autonomy & all
Turned to use. The fine economy of means.
All the tensions. All the final lessons.
Stuck it to the DCS 100 Carnivore. Loaded it
In Io-Storm & Oompah Omnivore. A jukebox
Set to play a tune: *Take us to the moon*. Listen to
The IOUs rocking out the actionable blues.
When Brain was uploaded out at old Saint Liz.
Encoded by the goaded and the criminally insane.
Where they used to pay society their Io dues.

Where once there was a man invoked the muse.

# Three Russian Anecdotes
*After listening to Maxim Kantor*

1.

And when American philanthropists
Got excited about the new Russian reforms
A group of them sent to impoverished
Towns and villages on the Siberian tundra
Enough copies of Solzhenitsyn's *Gulag
Archipelago* for each illiterate citizen.

2.

And when the new Russian reforms
Produced only the Oligarchs
And KGB colonels running the show
You frequently saw in Moscow
Starving veterans of World War II
Selling their medals to tourists.

3.

And when the new leaders
Had no more notion than Brezhnev
What to do with the vast population
Without any work or hope or ideas
They eventually said: You're free.
With the new Russian reforms you
Can run in the race with the rest of
The world: Alas, they had no legs.

# Longs and Shorts

*(For Roy Fisher at 80)*


And will a photograph save us? We're old enough
To have had a temptation to think
That the old cliché about *ars longa* had some
Actual merit. What's long
Are the drifting sands as we plod to the
Music of *vita brevis*. But it *is* a music, tra-la.
It seems but a moment ago you were only 70
And we urged you in your words to
*Put the piano at risk*, to left-hand us a poem.
But photography's the democratic art.
I just saw a snap of you in South Bend, Indiana
The very night of your reading in 1980.
It was also the first night you'd spent outside
Of Britain: Not in Paris, not in Rome, but
South Bend, Indiana. I can't even say it's the
Midwestern Birmingham, although you
Liked and found familiar the "abandoned workings,"
As W.H. Auden would say, of the old
Studebaker auto plant. After the reading we
Travelled out to the house of a prof
In the same car with another guest of the school
Who seemed even more laid-back
Than you, though also a bit incongruous.
He too both wrote and put the piano at risk. He too
Had a cosmopolitan soul. At the party
You sat together on a sofa—clearly someone
Would play. As you jazzed the *vita brevis*
Out of the upright, *Ars Longa* himself
Appeared with his camera. And here in
A short book is the picture long after the music
Has fled. I can see it's my friend Roy Fisher
Fishing for the right notes in a riff.
But the caption grasping at by god immortal life
Declaims like Caesar's newsboy: *John Cage
Plays four minutes of silence*

While on the opposite page Harold Brodkey's
Mislabeled *Joseph Brodsky*.
Irreversible, Roy. But what the hell?

# Interlinear Dialogue with a Poem Found with Letters from Göran Printz-Påhlson

So, at last, there is one thing we have in common
The habit of assuaging the country mist:
*But reading here about it I'm not sure at all if I'm to*
*Find the mist in country outside of Malmö, or Cambridge,*
*Or for that matter in the country just beyond South Bend,*
*An Indiana town you rather inexplicably*
*Enjoyed. Nor can I be sure, squinting at an old-fashioned*
*Carbon copy on an old-fashioned onion skin,*
*If this "assuaging" should occur*
Because there is one thing we must not allow,
In particular in the autumn when the
Pastures are trivial, leaves playful,
*Or, if we did allow this thing, just what the consequences*
*Might become. This is how I figure: a description*
Of any kind of narrative (as I a daughter
Asleep from drinking, left alone), *a narrative that must,*
*We suppose, have something to do with "trivial" pastures*
*And "playful" leaves, as well as with the afore-*
*Mentioned "assuaging" of the country mist. But "as I a daughter"?*
*It certainly wakes one up, even from a narrative*
*Not properly described. And does one, GPP, "describe"*
*A narrative, even "(as I a daughter,*
*Asleep from drinking, left alone)"? Or just get on with telling?*
*I sometimes used to leave*
*You alone, asleep from drinking, in the Clare Hall*
*Common room after lunch. That would have been in 1976-7,*
*Year of our collaboration, a memory*
*That makes me wonder, too, if*
*This is not a self-translation from the Swedish,*
*Something that you often did, as in the case, for instance,*
*Of the famous "When Beaumont and Tocqueville First Visited*
*Sing-Sing," a poem which still, I understand,*
*Causes problems for your editors: Put it in*
*The "Poems in Swedish" section, or later on, page 85 ff,*
*The "Poems in English" part?—since*
This is the time I don't come from
But rather the opposite, like St. Augustine,

Another installment in my debt to you
My darling Janet. *I do, I think, remember Janet, or*
*Maybe I confuse that name with Annette, who woke us both*
*From time to time when we were feeling "rather the*
*Opposite," like St. Augustine, therefore both incurring*
*An installment in our debt.* Negation NEGATION
*Sounds apocalyptic when at least you can speak and say*
At least I can speak now and not
At that omen (I was a poet once and
Then) miraculously (read an old
Acquaintance. *Who was that? And why does this*
*Parenthesis not close? I'm glad to speak now too, but*
*Why not "at that omen"? (To the omen, through the omen,*
*For the omen, five the omen, six?)*
*Are you a poet here, or only once (upon a time)*
*And then. When—Oh Miracle!— an old acquaintance*
*Came up riding with a text in writing saying*
*"Read an old acquaintance for your sins!" And isn't this the IS*
That is first-order logic when
Consensually agreed on, or words to that effect?
That is why this poem is called "The
Decline of the Supernatural," although its
Title is "On What Was As Near To
Happiness," or "Interlinear Dialogue with a Poem
Found with Letters from Printz-Påhlson"
But dedicated to Henry Mayhew
And the memory of Clive Jenkins.
*School children will require a gloss or so, a moss*
*Or so beneath a tree out somewhere in the country where*
*They might lie down and dream, assuaging mist.*
*The open parenthesis runs on. A gap of space, a hiss:*
I do only countenance arithmetical order
Which is the stark nonsequitur of most
Vengeful fathers. *Line break and page break: then*
Forgive me, as vulgar as a poem mentioning Chomsky
(*Where, exactly?*) incognito there,
Or whales,     or wage demands     *may be*

# Postcards from the Sofa,

*Which my mother used to call a Davenport*

\*

*Re. trails, paths, ley lines, stagecoach routes*

Fourier was another road man—
    the phalansteries were to be connected
by roads patrolled by children on quaggas
    and zebras, with names like *The Sunflower Horde*.
The streets of the phalanstrey were to be policed
    by girls and sissies on ponies
handing out demerits for bad grammar and
    scruffy flower beds.

\*

*Re. Claims that the Sheela-na-gig figure over Whittlesford church door is an image of Gogmagog, T.C. Lethbridge argues that words like goggle, giggle, ogle, and the child's grotesque toy Golliwog are all verbal derivations.*

Begging Lethbridge's pardon, but *goggle*
    is the frequentive of *gig*
(as in gig-lamp, the two lights on a buggy or carriage).
    *Giggle* is the frequentive of *gag*.
Perhaps Bonnie Jean and I should publish our random
    Study of frequentives (*stab/staple*,
*Stop/stopper*, *tag/toggle*) which we use as a word
    game while waiting for trains.

\*

*Re. John Adams' opera 'Nixon in China'*

So: opera is a decade behind the short story. Adams
    gets $100,000; the production
costs $500,000. One of the things I love about our calling
    is that we work with paper and pencil.

I got $30 for my *Nixon*. But I offer his trip as the completion
    of Columbus's voyage to Cathay, on Vincian
apparatuses, and with Gertrude and Alice
    (retrograde foragers going back to where
it all started, to move forward again).

\*

*Re. the collaboration between Hedy Lemarr and George Antheil*
*On spread-spectrum technology*

The George Antheil info is something I've astonished
    people with for 40 years, not that
anybody believed it of Hedy, and they'd of course
    never heard of Antheil. I didn't know
about its extent to cell phones.

Cell phones allow 11-year-olds on European school
    tours to share their experience
with the folks back home. A friend's son called
    from the Vatican. "Hey Mom!
We've seen eight dead popes this morning."

\*

*Re. Poltonizing*

A useful word Bonnie Jean and I made from
    Austin Freeman's perfect factotum
Polton. I forget when I last wrote: we were in Denmark
    and Sweden at the butt of the summer.

Tennyrate, they've given me a MacArthur—even
    after I wrote them saying that I
never apply for or accept grants. They assumed I
    Didn't mean *them*.

I wonder if Picasso Poltonized. He did say
    "If rich, live poor."
Maybe that's my short-range solution

\*

*Re. Protestants in France*

I am, by the way, one of the Huguenots who
    escaped, in persona great-grandpa
on my mother's side. A particular frisson one
    afternoon, when Bonnie and I
were drinking Cocas in Bordeaux, Place Gambetta,
    and the *culte baptiste* came and preached
a sermon at all us sinners (various middle-aged
    women having their tea, two Brits
out of Graham Greene, a few teenagers). Lordy,
    to be so far from South Carolina
and still be pestered by Baptists!

\*

*Re. the poetry of Geoffrey Hill*

Imagine anybody being influenced by Allen Tate!

\*

*Re. his correspondent being from Ohio*

Do you know my little quatrains:

    France is my watchlight
    England is my tree,

Spain is my city wall
My sword is Italy.

Ireland's my strong arm
Germany my word,
Ohio my heart's love,
And prophecy my Lord

*

*Re. Having confused the herbs on his shelf*

Must run. I just realized the ground cinnamon
    I stirred into my coffee
was actually a half-teaspoon of turmeric!

*From the correspondence of Guy Davenport*

IV

# The Plumber

*For Jeffrey Dierbeck, because he asked*

I think it must have been Auden who said
That it's not even a contest between
The plumbers and the poets should you think for a moment
And ask: Which breed has brought to civilization
The most—noodlers of Apollo
Or the sons of Aquarius? Plumbers win hands down!
Think of the running open sewers of medieval towns,
Think of the flooded basements, the outhouse in the woods
Even in my grandparents' day. *Gardyloo* they'd shout
In London as they tipped the pisspot out on passersby.
Although I found it picturesque to pump the water
From a well at summer camp, I thought the sulfur tasted
Infernal—and, older and elsewhere, I might have nodded
In agreement with the engineer of Pompeii's aqueduct
When he knew before all others that something dreadful
Was afoot, answering a call from some Roman grandee
*En vacances* who bitched that his water smelled like hell.

Jeff, I've called you out both day and night for
Everything from leaking pipes to plugged up drains
For something like a quarter of a century.
When the upstairs tub crashed through the ceiling
Landing in the downstairs sink, you rebuilt my house.
The water ran again. We drank. We bathed.
Shall I paint your portrait in heroic terms? Why not?
The hero is a man who saves you from a situation
Where you cannot save yourself. When the great boiler
In our hundred year old house—a boiler just
As old as the foundation—began to shake and rumble
Like a nuclear power plant in meltdown, you shouted
Through the basement door *Get the hell upstairs*
And then came down yourself and did your magic just
Before, you told me later, it was going to burst.
I once told you, I think, about a famous woman poet
Reading poems at Notre Dame about the boy friend

Who'd dumped her that included the line
*Anyway, you were a bad plumber.* Nothing worse
Than that, she implied. As she read on in her poem
Everyone could hear the nun in the first row suddenly
Saying *Oh!*—and giggling as she finally got the joke.

That was part of a conversation I remember well
After another problem had been solved and we chatted over
Beers about one thing and another and you praised
For the first time, as you have many times since,
The Traditional Crafts. You're no sentimentalist
So I won't say you got all misty over that. But I could
Sense your solidarity with carpenters and potters,
Electricians, stone cutters . . . maybe even poets . . .
Although there's no real analogy between the infinitely
Delicate descent of the great Aqua Augusta
And, let us say, measures in the prosody of Virgil,
Some hopeful poet still might want to force it anyway.
I myself heard Tony Harrison and Robert Lowell talk
All night about heroic couplets, at dawn agreeing
That their favorites were in Dryden's *Aureng-Zebe*, where
Lines hold their own with "the pouring of whole rivers."
The talk had been so technical, Tony later said, he felt
That he and Lowell had been two plumbers at their trade,
Measuring dimensions and materials of a thousand pipes,
Fitting them for use. I don't know if I can borrow *use*
In any way from you for what I do, but I know from
Observation of your efficacious labors all these years
That when you say *The water will run here*
                                        —it does.

# My House at 100
*[To be read at a hearing before the Chapin Park Historic Preservation Commission]*

> *My house is older than Henry;*
> *That's fairly old.*
>                     John Berryman, Dream Song 385

Its capitals have landed me
In court . . . Scamozzis
Made of local mud and horse hair
Cracked and fell apart. I thought
Some Dorics would be fine, but
Found photographers and Commissar
Of gabled roofs and porches
With a summons for the one who,
Ignorant of ordinance, had violated
Rules of exclusion that pertain
To stoops or patios or steps including
Handrails balusters and columns
Tiles decorations and, indeed,
The capitals.
            Oh Queen Anne,
Bless us with eclectic
Tolerance. For who's to say just
When were added the Scamozzis as there
Are no pictures before 1926?
Prohibited: any change to the essential
Character as seen from street
By adding features or unsightly
Fixtures. But my Dorics, Frau Professor,
Are most sightly—also modest, made
Of wood. Go arrest un-anodized
Aluminum across the street. Go
Get Mr. Siding. I intend no
Disrespect. In fact I side with you
In giving back to this old neighborhood
Some side and History.
It's your hysterical and rude
Aggression has me hamstrung in this
Matter, Madam, to the point

I would invoke the Potawatomis
From whom your forbears stole this
Property and built eventually
Your District with its secret laws
Against the Dorians themselves
Who spring to life and my defense
Invoked as manitus
In French-Ojibwa or Algonquian—
Languages without the word
*Scamozzi*. More than that
The mandate for your capitals
Of preference indicates
An outlay of about
$1,000 each for the ceramics,
Made to order, so you say, in
California. That I can't afford.
Besides, my wife
Is English and she knows
Queen Anne herself. Also Queen
Elizabeth, of whom you may have read.
Also Queen of Hearts.
Off, I say, My Lady,
With your bureaucratic head.

# Not Quite

I think I ought to tell Muldoon
About the roundabout outside South Bend—
The streets lead to a village called Pantoum—
And you can circle on it without end.

About the roundabout outside South Bend
They say there used to be a traffic light
That held commuters up without an end,
Sitting in their cars all through the night

And staring at that traffic light
That seemed eternally to hold on red.
The cars sat there all through the night
And nobody got home to bed.

Six ways that light would flash out red
And if you prayed or shouted *green*
And hoped you might get home to bed
In code the light flashed: *Tough, Paudeen,*

However much you prayed for green.
But then an engineer, Calhoun,
Who hoped to get them home to bed
Designed a roundabout, dragooned

Yet other engineers. Calhoun's
Idea was to build a kind of installation,
Like the Irish roundabout at Dragoon
Station, to relieve the consternation

With a kind of built up distillation
Of the drivers' meditation upon *dearth* and *doom*.
Stationed! to relieve their consternation,
Homeward bound to old Pantoum.

I think I ought to tell Muldoon.

# At the Metropolitan

*(Overheard as a school group passes by)*

Did you see all those baby butts on wings
And that Pousant (one says) where things
Got raunchy—satires looking down on Venus
Clutching at her shaven *mind veneris*

As it's called by our poor old Miss Mundt?
She ran us right on past the cunt
By that Courbet (he rhymes it with the Met).
It's like a porn show on the internet

Except that no one moves. And there's a penis
Or maybe it's a dildo that, between us,
Dido really liked more than Aeneas.

Time to go. If there were one more show
I'd like that Warhol guy, down low
Up high. Out of here & just go with the flow.

# Meditation and Conversation at 2 a.m.

So we used to have problems
And now we have *issues*. But I have problems
With issues. The economy is not an issue,
It's a problem. So is the noise coming from your car.

And *individuals* used to be called people, even
Men and women. Are you the person
Keeping me awake with the speakers blaring
In your car? Do you have an issue with that?

You ask. I do. I know that your music is awesome—
That is, not bad, fairly cool—but the individuals
Living here need sleep. You and your partner?
My wife and I. And do you know what's *awesome*?

What's awesome? Standing high in the Alps
In a storm, first looking into Chapman's Homer,
Sitting down to read *King Lear* again. That's neat.
No, that's Keats. Are he and Chapman

Partners? If one individual is much older, that's
Perhaps a problem for them both. The one who hit the homer,
I suppose was older, running round the bases, stout,
Just to stare way out, pacific. They were both just folks.

Homeowners stuck with one of those sub-primes?
Sublime. You've got it. They had real issues.
And you guys live right here? We do, and try to sleep at night.
So fine, I'll turn the music down. All right.

# Smoking Poem

*Sing sweetly for tobacco. Anon. madrigal*

It seemed then that everybody smoked. Parents,
Teachers, tough guys on playgrounds, maybe even
Girls who maybe wouldn't tell but nonetheless lit up
At home when no one was around. Movie stars.

Especially movie stars. Gable with his hand
Cupped around a fag peering from a poster
Advertising some dumb film, the smoke
Curling artfully around his face. Marilyn. Jane.

But also intellectuals: Sartre with his Gauloises,
Auden and Camus; Bertrand Russell and his pipe.
Others smoked cigars: Churchill, for example.
FDR bit down upon a fancy holder like a bit.

Later, "Johnny" on the new TVs: *Call For Philip
Morris. LSMFT: Lucky Strike means fine tobacco.*
Every home had ashtrays full of stubs, even ours.
Lighters made nice gifts. Kools were very cool.

Make it with a Marlborough man. Before dinner,
After sex, between the bath and new party dress.
Everybody smoked. Although he doesn't say so,
Stevens' lady in the peignoir smoked a cigarette.

Bill Williams' *pure products of America* & Williams
Too, who should have known, being a physician,
That it would be the death of us. But what, otherwise,
Do with our hands? Steal things? Masturbate?

Everything important went with smoke: Gossip,
Assignations, business meetings, long walks at night
With a friend, criminal plots, police interrogations,
Jazz in storefront clubs, Brando on the waterfront.

Then it stopped. Atmosphere would never be
The same. How to say you loved her without
First giving her a light? Her long drag. Your own.
How else contend a little with the dark.

# For an Old Actor Exploited at the Awards

That trick they played on you
at the Oscar show was obscene—
getting you as a weak old man to play
the part of a stereotypical Senile Cit
in a terrible geezer joke about old men.
You could barely walk with a cane, barely
speak with your stroked-out voice.
And you let them match you up with a
nubile girl, who smirked when you
pinched her arm (on cue) and gave her
(also on cue) a lecherous look. What
they deserved for this was to have had
you drop down dead right there—fall
with a soft thud onto the carpet that
led from the wings into the heaven of
bright lights and bright stars. They beeped
The F-word OK when Ms. Silicon Boobs
stuttered it into the f, f, f, face
of k, k, k, king for a day, but you could have
fucked them right enough with an act
that no one could possibly follow.

*For Kirk Douglas*

# Rostropovich at Aldeburgh

### I As Soloist

The Haydn Concerto in C with Britten's cadenzas:
He flies through these (the cadenzas)
Like an Aeroflot plane, like a Concordsky,
Out of the eighteenth century into our own
And then back.
It's difficult for us to tell
Which of these ages he's happiest in
Or with which composer:
Or whether if all of us wore our wigs
And our wings
To tea at the Maltings
We'd feel completely out of our time
Or merely well dressed.


### II As Conductor

The Shostakovich 14th.
Which broods on
Death and is eloquent.

His wife, Galina Vishnevskaya,
Sings with Ulrik Cold
The texts by Apollinaire, Lorca,

Kuchelbecker, and Rilke.
Which brood on
Death and are eloquent.

The widow of the composer
Sits in the audience.
What we applaud for is what

In each of us might, if we're lucky,
Survive. And he applauds back at us,
Being Russian. He's beaming and

Bouncing, blessing us all with his smile.
He kisses the hand of his wife,
The cheek of the first violinist,

The balding head of every balding
Percussionist:
One, two, three, and four.

# To a Fraud Whose Work Has Come to Be Canonical

Now all the lies are told
go public and seek praise
as prizes now unfold
like afternoons on days
dishonor schemes in groves
and shame lurks in the eyes
and lips can only love
a self which they contrive.

Born to charm and born
for easy triumph, turn
this way and like some
weeping thing amid a field
of bones, anthologize despair
and cry at last *Forlorn*!
because in all this barren yield
there is no living air.

# The Cotranslator's Dilemma

Again the e-mail draft appears on my screen.
I go back to work.
Tranströmer's successor speaks aloud from his poem.
Sort of, that is. I'm supposed to make such improvements
that everyone in America will recognize at a flash
the original style & voice, the very personality of this poet
known up to now only by his most intimate friends.
I despair. They are waiting in Lund for my version.
But it's already in English, so what should I do?
I change an article: "*The* cow in the pasture" would really
be better written here "*A* cow in the pasture."
I stare at the screen. Maybe a comma just before the conjunction.
At just that moment I hear a commotion in the hall.
I can hear several people questioning students:
Which is the charlatan's office? I recognize the Swedish accents.
Suddenly Jesper and Leif, Göran and Lars-Håkan
all tumble into my room. We're here to help you, they laugh.
Göran offers me a virtual beer.
The heart of your problem, Leif says in Swedish,
Is that you don't know Swedish. What?
He says in English: The problem is you don't know Swedish.
Oh, that. Well, I work from this other guy's drafts.
What do you do? He seems to have a whole list of questions.
I show him the screen: "*A cow*" was once "*The cow*," I say,
and commas, or their absence, are very important.
That's it? he asks. Nothing else?
Well, there's the issue of prepositions. I find that most
Of my Swedish colleagues get confused:
A poet whose head is up in the clouds may appear with
his head up *around* the clouds, or up *about* the clouds,
or even up *from* or up *off* the clouds!
The four Swedes sputter with amusement or contempt.
So that's all? Articles, prepositions and commas?
Well, sometimes, if I'm lucky.
And what if you're not? Not lucky, that is.
Ah, then—I hesitate—then I have to rewrite the poem.

You'd re-write somebody's poem?
Not in Swedish, of course, I hasten to say. Just in English.
Ah well, they grumble, that's a relief.
I mean, what can you do with a poem set entirely in Lapland
that's full of *yoiks* or *voulles*? And then he throws in
classical myths and quotes not only from Sappho but also Rimbaud.
American readers will never sort it all out.
American readers could learn to yoik for themselves, Jesper insists.
In this poem with a cow? I mean, I say,
in the poem that appeared on my screen containing *the* cow.
The one whose poet had his head up around the clouds.
Apollo and Hermes are also, I can see, there on the screen,
and what am I to do with words like *Poikilóthronos* and *Boukólos*?
Well, Lars-Håkan says, what *will* you do?
I'll change the setting entirely, move the lot of them to Texas!
But in Texas nobody yoiks, everyone protests.
There are plenty of cows, however, and cowboys like to yell & shout
While they ride all around saying things like *Yahoo*!
But a Yoik is a Lapland poem, it's a chant, an incantation, a song!
In my Texas version the cowboys will sing quite a lot:
*Git along little dogie*, and stuff like that.
That's the line in fact that I'll substitute for the quote from Rimbaud.
What about Hermes? What about Apollo?
I think I'll exchange them for John Wayne & Clint Eastwood.
Those are mythic types American readers relate to.
All the Swedes have now stopped grinning & laughing
and are starting to cry, tearing their hair.
In Greek plays lots of people cry and tear their hair.
That's another thing that gets into this poem, along with the
language itself: the *Poikilóthronoses* and *Boukóloses*.
Sounds like some bacteria infecting the meat of the burger.
Göran says, darting a knowing glance over at Jesper:
The author of this poem is an eminent Hellenist!
By God, I thought he was a Swede!
Anyway, if you've got to have your Greek go see Ezra Pound.
He's long dead, of course, which means

you might as well just go on working with me.
I've become a little tipsy by this point drinking the virtual beer
and suddenly drop the nearly empty virtual bottle onto the keyboard.
Yoiks! We're all at once transported off to Amazon.com
The Amazon: Now that's better than Texas!
The stern-wheeler is sailing upriver from Santarém.
Elizabeth Bishop is getting on board, clutching
an empty wasp's nest given to her by the druggist
in the town's little blue pharmacy. I follow her with my cow
which has somehow attracted a herd—
not of cattle exactly, but of sheep, goats, yaks,
chickens, llamas, cats and yellow dogs.
What's going on? I'm not exactly sure, but I like it.
Jesper's shouting in English: Who do you think you are,
some kind of Hercules? That poem (that golden girdle!) is mine;
I, I, I, am Tranströmer's successor!
Not any more, I exclaim, heading into the current
on the riverboat called *Poikilóthronos Juan*.
Off in wintry Lund, all the systems start to crash.
Every screen flickers and goes blank.

# Stalin as Wolf

The position of the wolf was once secure in political theory
before it was driven by urbanization back to that final wilderness,
e.g. Siberia, where it lingers still without, to anyone's notice,
affecting contemporary politics. The plains sparkle in sunlight
as a helicopter rushes over the landscape: stunted birches
appear and disappear out on the snow covered tundra
where all at once a wolf can be seen: it runs, it trips,
looks backward: someone has edited-in the hot gasps
of a dog to make us hear its fear: it is filmed close-up
and the camera is slightly jarred when the helicopter gunner
fires. The wolf is hit, rolls over in a swirl of snow,
then everything is still. Every year in the Soviet Union
more than 22,000 wolves were killed according to recent
statistics, and perhaps it is even yet a silent requirement
of Russian polity—menacing, inaccessible—which would explain
the cynical, obsessive precision of the hunting methods
both in the filmed sequence noted above, which,
with no comment, introduced a documentary on modern Siberia,
and also on the inner tundra where the wolf howls with hunger
in a nightmare only partially reclaimable. The facts about wolves
in Sweden at my disposal allow no conclusions, and yet,
within its territory, the wolf has developed local, independent
clans which have been identified as distinctive species. About
the role of the wolf in Russian politics 1875–1953, however,
we know more than we suppose: Stalin's most wolf-like characteristic
was distrust, which grew in proportions never foreseen by classical
lupine theory. As early as in Aesop we can find sufficient examples
to maintain that Stalin's role in political theory is basic:
the Wolf as Butcher, masters to perfection the partition technique
which is the base of political equality. The jaws of the wolf
equal the Knife, and classical myth provides again the scenario
which ought to have haunted us earlier: hunting the Wolf became
in the Thirties a dominant trait in Soviet politics; he who wrote
"All power to the Soviets" three years before Kronstadt was now
the uncontested Butcher, the principle of absolute mistrust
had triumphed over Equality and the pack closed ranks around Stalin

in the whirling snowstorm. The Bolsheviks had certainly planned
an equitous banquet of wolves, but forgotten the moment when Knife
turns into Weapon and the feast into its opposite. The gasps
haunt me, the plains sparkle, the film invades the memory:
am I willing to test that project now when Stalin's crimes
are rostered and surveyed, now when his blood-thirst, along with
the prospects which made it possible, have all been analysed?
Zoologists can emend, on essential points, classical mythology,
refract the Stalinoid language: lacking both project and theory
the pack makes real the apothegm: "To each according to his need,
from each according to his ability." It refutes the picture
that pursues me and, in the end, obliges me to abandon
my language: gazing at Stalin, letting the wolf run off.

*By Jesper Svenbro;*
*Translated with Göran Printz-Påhlsson*

# Göran Printz-Påhlson: Two Poems

**Sir Charles Babbage Returns to Trinity College** *After Having Commissioned the Swedish Mechanic Scheutz to Build a Difference Engine. On the Bank of the River Cam He Gazes at the Bridge of Sighs and Contemplates the Life of the Dragonfly*

No man can add an inch to his height, says the Bible. Yet once I saw the detective Vidocq change his height by circa an inch and a half. It has always been my experience that one ought to maintain the greatest accuracy even in the smallest things.

No one has taught me more than my machine. I know that a law of nature is a miracle. When I see the dragonfly, I see its nymph contained in its glittering flight. How much more probable it is that any one law will prove to be invalid than it will prove to be sound. It must happen in the end: although the wheels and levers all move accurately enough, the *other* number will appear, the unexpected, the incalculable, when the nymph bursts into a dragonfly. I see a hand in life, the unchanging hand of The Great Effacer.

Therefore be scrupulous and guard your reason, in order that you may recognize the miracle when it occurs. I wrote to Tennyson that his information was incorrect when he sang "every minute dies a man, / Every minute one is born." In fact, every minute one and one-sixteenth of a man is born. I refuse to abandon this one-sixteenth of a man.

*Translated with the author*

## Man-Made Monster Surreptitiously Regarding Idyllic Scene *in Swiss Hermitage, a Copy of Goethe's 'Werther' Resting in its Lap*

It is sometimes considered to be an advantage to start from scratch. I myself would be the first to admit that my maker did a good job when he constructed my brain, although it must be said that he was unsuccessful with my outer appearance: my ongoing programme of self-education has provided me with many a happy hour of intellectual satisfaction. Spying on these touching family tableaux unobserved makes me nevertheless both excited and dejected. I suspect that only with the greatest of difficulties shall I myself be able to establish meaningful relationships with other beings. It is not so much my disfigured countenance which distresses me—I have accustomed myself to *that* by gazing at it in a nearby tarn and now find it, if not immediately attractive, then, at least, captivating: in particular the big screws just under my ears which my maker insisted on putting there for God knows what purpose, accentuate my expression of virile gravity and ennui—as rather a certain lack of elegance and animal charm. It seems for instance to be almost impossible for me to find a suit that fits as it should. One of my more casual acquaintances, a certain Count Dracula, whom I vaguely remember having encountered in some circumstances or other—regrettably I cannot remember where or when—is in this respect much more fortunate: I envy him his relaxed manner of deporting himself in evening dress, but I have to admit that I cannot understand the reason for his negative (and extremely selfish) attitude to his environment. For myself, it seems as if my background and construction limit the possibilities for the successful development of my personality in socially acceptable forms. Evidently, I must choose between two possible careers: either to seek self-expression in the pursuit of crime—within which vast and varied field of activity sexual murder ought to offer unsurpassed opportunities for a creature of my disposition—or during my remaining years quietly to warm my hands at the not altogether fantastically blazing but nonetheless never entirely extinguished fires of scholarship.

*Translated with the author*

# V

# The HIJ

# The Hijofit

1. Haphazard

        is the method of the new hussars;
the tsar's unhappy; bless him

and applause aplenty bring to his tsarina.
All bells toll this inauspicious hour.

Peasant absentee shuns orthodoxy of
the Bishop of Pah. It reigns down from clouds

O hallelujah crowd and ever after: Winds blow
across the steppe, the messenger

caught up in mass and mission
fails in the individual soul: Everything's for sale,

especially oil, soil. Ahph! Our brother's pipeline
sabotaged by cabbage claims. Borscht!

Poetics is no longer worth a pension
even for a splaygirl in from Budapest. Anapests—

the three red accents on her breasts.
Hazard me a guess, dauntless guest of hap-

penstance drinking vodka at our happy hour.
That was the moment. That was the power.

Hapax Legoman was his love, who
drove a nine and twenty for her dower.

2. INDENTURE

        is indefinite to articles;
Madame is indecent; *any* we might say enough?

Or *some* things. Her dayglo spikeheel shoes
are on, although her clothes are off.

On-off. As though one clicked a light switch
several times. Or in-out. He wrote for

the dispatch but wasn't articled in *n.2:* a contract
or a deed; *tr.v*: to bind in function of

derivative: $\int f(x)dx + C$ where C's the arbitrary
constant. She did indeed love *me* though *he*

sought indemnity for integrals
where $\int f(x)dx$ was any member of her set.

The poems they wrote to her about her
index of refraction! No one knew she was

indebted to the tsar. She was indicative.
Indelibles suggest an assignation with the prince,

the princess, and the handsome slave.
In the end she was

        indented   &indicted everywhere
courting nine and twenty to her grave.

3. Jerkwater

       town's the home of Jeroboam
who is aquarius to every passing phantom train.

Houses are jerrybuilt and shake like Jericho
when jayhawker nightfreights come arumbling through.

The Jews, the Gentiles there. The arbitrary constant C
was married to an Imam, tsar and all

his retinue forgotten. It was far away.
*Jesuits are exiled to Australia—to Jarvis Bay,*

*you Jerk!* said Mr. Waters. Indenture and Haphazard
were his favorite words. Herds of Yahwists

streaming toward Jerusalem and jet set derivatives
of *∫f(x)dx* expired in a desert without wells.

*I'm well enough*, said Jeroboam, *thank you very much*.
Ahph! Borsht! They should have come by train

where hallelujah crowd and everafter jerk
their waters to attain the wherewithal for steam.

Spare us any jeremiad. Everything's explained
by a damned outrageous jealousy:

Hapax Legoman more a Jezebel than Judith,
nine and twenty for a faithless C.

# The Defitcit

1. Deficient

      and degenerate, the Hij was defrauded
by Defiance. HIJ: he liked to go by his initials like

the FDRs and JFKs, although he was Republican.
Republic was deformed when the Hij was out

beyond the limit of his sums: broken definite integral
left him no degrees. It pained him and

he called on: Defoe, de Gaulle, Degas, et. al. But they
weren't any help at all. Afph! Borsht!

They'd degrade his forces with artillery and fix
bayonets to break his squares, but he was pretty cool:

All roots were cubed in his ice tray. *Just water, Hij,*
said A.J. Haphazard. *I'll defray your costs if*

*You return the article you took from my degree.*
Thee and Thou were both defrocked

before arriving here and now so wholly *dégagé*.
They'd defer the whole damned thing

provided biwings weren't already in the air
defoliating forests, model nine and twenty firing

tracers over Jerkwater's vast degaussing works.
The last definition: "Busted Billionaire."

2. EIDOLONIE

        was elected by an acclamation
as "the most likely to succeed," although she

neither spelled properly nor could pronounce
the name of their assembly: *Eisteddfod*.

Ilya Grigorievich, Dwight David, Karl Adolf: all
filled in the Es, as did Alexander Gustave.

Eiger Alp is taller than the Eiffel Tower by some
12,000 feet. Eidolonie said: *you may ejaculate, my dear,*

*but don't come to my place.* Her lover was eidetic,
E.D. Eidetic, his E.T.C. irregular

as waves rolled in at two or three megahertz
above the atmosphere on Elba,

the E layer breaking up a classified transmission
all through the Tuscan Archipelago.

The Hij was no Napoleon although he always
kept his right hand in his shirt, sent

his mail ewards, took care to use the secret moniker
as *nom de guerre*, drawing out

his nine and twenty to defend the honor of a lady
he knew nothing yet about.

3. Facsimile

        was no part of that faction, although
he went to meetings once.

Eidolonie said he was forgotten, but that was just
a ruse to get him off the factory floor.

What a factor he become; complete fabrication of the Hij
and sourced in many fabliaux, he was a facer

when it came to ascertaining his intent. He was more
factitious than facetious in the end, and that

enabled penetration of their code. Oh, his secret was
his love for Eidolonie, his posture on

the postage stamp a provocation had it not said
E.D. Eidetic underneath the photograph.

His face, alas, looked quite aristocratic, so they
broke his nose and cut off all his hair.

He was an heir to the ages. That's why they hated him.
They hatted him with bowler first and then

with *bonnet rouge*. His original eventually was lost
among the more than ninety facets

of the compound insect eye with which they stared
at him: bent and starved and only twenty nine.

# The Nopofit

1. NONENTITY

        would nonchalantly noodle nomagraphs
of straight and curved where Z squared

was equal to his height times weight plus breath,
a malfeasance of the *prima fascia*. *Hij*, he'd say,

*You nonpareil, don't call me square Z when
I'm your own nonillionth for the nonce, the best*

*damn non sequitur in town.* His mother had him
singing l-m-n-o-p when he was two. He asked

her for the "alpaphet song." First she'd sing it,
then he'd have of go. *Enupofit* he'd finally say,

and then she'd mop his drooling gob. The Hij
wiped the floor with him, cleaned his clock,

locked him nightly in the fridge. He couldn't any longer
stand the look of him, and kicked him

with a square boot of ten. *Fuckin' Nopofit you
nonentity*, he'd say. *Now I understand why*

*your mother baked you in a pie. Heave-ho
me ice cube, hot stuff at only two,*

*at twenty pretty cool*—a nomination to the nines,
nonesuch assassin and the ides a go.

2. Onomastic

        was a Greek who ran the diner where the Hij
did his deals among Russkies and the Polish bards.

Oneiromancy, one-night-stands, and
one-up-manship were deals. The Greek was meant to

name them but he couldn't find the port of Nakhodka
on the map or part with nabobs in his clientele.

The Hij hedged his bets on ontology and waited
for ontogeny to recapitulate phylogeny. Nabobs didn't

know the difference between *O* and *Oh*, but the onus
was on all the oligarchs who also gathered at

the dining place committing onanistic acts in
coffee cups when O's pretty waitress stripped right down

to bra and little thong and murmured *Oh!*
This gave the Hij an opening to intervene on his ophicleide.

Everyone was so opinionated. *O!* said the Polish master,
baiting Greek and oligarch, Hij and nabob,

nonentity and nonpareil, *Don't you know the difference
between a caught breath of surprise and a long breath*

*of wonder? Nine to twenty are the odds, O my even Ohs,
that it's Aoi or an ogle in your next cynghanedd.*

3. Plastered

        in their local and unlikely Jerkwater pub,
Facsimile, Nonentity, Haphazard, and the Hij

continued buying one another pints.
They'd moved on from the greasy Grecian spoon

once they heard that Planck (Max) was constant
and Plantagenet out at their plantation.

Gypsum cement, hemi-hydrated cal of sulfate, all
were plantigrade of foot when not plangent otherwise

On ophicleides or circulating in the planetary nebula.
The Hij thought he was immortal as the Pleiades

but still was enamored of the Eidolon whose lover he
had lofted to the Eigon Alp. Poor old good old Hij.

Ahpf! Borsht! He missed his sentimental meetings with
The Bishop of Pah. *Jerkwater's the limit*, he was

heard to say. *Thank you Jeroboam. I may be a plaster cast
but I am still the boss. Bastard of a plasmagene at payoff,*

*I'm also Pliny with a pistol on a plinth. Evolved from
the Pliocene, I am here to stay.*

*Measure me a nine-and-twenty, plimsolls off in May:
Dummkopffts on double-docket, dizened for today.*

# Epilogue: The Hij's Happy Book of Insults

You're a Hindoo Haji Hoky Half-Cast Hun you Hippie
Hymie Jerry Jocky Kaffir Katsap Jigaboo

[big breath]

You Limey Lace Curtain Irish Mickey Mammy Moskal
Nig-nog Nip you Pakki Pancake Pepper

[breath]

Poncho Polack Pom you Redneck Redskin Sasquatch
Sambo Shiksa Skippy Slopehead Southern Fairy

[breath]

Spearchucker Taffy Tinker Towelheaded Uncle Tom
You Wog you Wap Albino Abbo Alligator bait

[breath]

You Ape you Argie Beaner Boche you Bog Irish Bohunk
Camel Jocky Charlie Chee-chee Chinaman

[breath]

You Cholo Coolie Coconut you Cunt-eyed Cracker Crow you
Jigarooni Dhoti Dink you Dutchman Eskimo you FreeState Flipnit

Greaseball Gringo Gypsy Beatnik Guido Gimp you

You . . . You . . .
Yoyo  Yankeedoodle Poet Parrot Jingo Jerk

You Wetback Anchorbaby Gimcrack Mayflower Mug

# Notes and Sources

From *Swimming at Midnight*, *Pages*, and *New Selected Poems*

## I

*Grimm's Fairy Tales*, trans. Margaret Hunt with an introduction by Frances Clark Sayers ('Not Having Heard a Single Fairy Tale'). Branko Miljković, 'Dok Budeš Pevao' ('While You Are Singing"). Ezra Pound, 'Cino' ('E.P. In Crawfordsville'). Osip Mandelstam, 'Lines on Stalin'; Nadezhda Mandelstam, *Hope Against Hope* ('Horace Augustus Mandelstam Stalin'). Cyrillic words and phrases as translated by Ivan Lalić from 'Friendship' into Serbian; the Serbian word in the first line is the title of the poem; the other Serbian words are my Christian name and surname ('Into Cyrillic'). Otto Bihalji-Merin and Alojz Benac, *Bogomil Sculpture*; Jacques Lacarrière, *The Gnostics* ('Bogomil in Languedoc' and 'The Silence of Stones'). Svetozar Koljević, *The Epic in the Making*; Albert B. Lord, *The Singer of Tales*; Rebecca West, *Black Lamb and Grey Falcon* ('The Singer of Tales'). Robert Hass, 'Letter to a Poet' and other poems from *Field Guide* ('On Rereading a Friend's First Book"). Blaise Cendrars, *Complete Poems*, trans. Ron Padgett; Federico García Lorca, *Poet in New York*, trans. Greg Simon and Steven F. White ('Two in New York' and 'Easter 1912 and Christmas 1929'). Edgar Rice, *Captain Sir Richard Francis Burton*; Charles Nicholl, *Somebody Else: Arthur Rimbaud in Africa*; Arthur Rimbaud, *Complete Works*, trans. Paul Schmidt ('Two in Harar'). Gertrude Bell, *The Desert and the Sown*; Janet Wallach, *Desert Queen* ('She Maps Iraq'). Anna Akhmatova, *My Half Centruy: Selected Prose*; Roberta Reeder, *Anna Akhmatova: Poet and Prophet* ('Six or So in Petersburg'). René Char, *Fureur et Mystère, Feuillets d'Hypnos*; Carrie Noland, *Poetry at Stake* ('Francophiles, 1958'). Letters of T.E. Lawrence to Kathleen Scott, Cambridge University Library archive; Louisa Young, *A Great Task of Happiness: The Life of Kathleen Scott* ('Some Letters').

## II

I should note that the 'Dedication to a Cycle of Poems on the Pilgrim Routes to Santiago de Compostela' was originally intended to initiate 'A Compostela Diptych,' the third and longest poem in my volume called *A Gathering of Ways*, which will appear again soon in my *Collected Longer Poems* from Shearsman. For a number of reasons it was not, finally, printed in that context. Nonetheless, I would like to acknowledge the original intention. The poems about music and composers in this section derive chiefly from the compositions themselves, the multi-volume *Grove Dictionary of Music*, *The Harvard Dictionary of Music*, CD liner notes, and the standard biographies. I should be more specific with regard to the poem on Arnold Schoenberg: Willi Reich, *Schoenberg: A Critical Biography*; H.H. Stückenschmidt, *Arnold*

*Schoenberg*; Alexander L. Ringer, *Arnold Schoenberg: The Composer as Jew*; Pamela Cooper-White, *Schoenberg and the God-Idea: The Opera 'Moses und Aron'*; Thomas Mann, *Doctor Faustus*; Gunilla Bergsten, *Thomas Mann's 'Doctor Faustus': The Sources and Structure of the Novel* ('Diminished Third'). 'Master Class' derives from Lotte Lehmann's *Eighteen Song Cycles: Studies in Their Interpretation*. The section on Schubert in 'Unfinished' derives from Christopher H. Gibbs' *The Life of Schubert*; those on Haydn's last quartets and Shostakovich's *The Gamblers* from liner notes to the Sony and BMG recordings. The remaining list of sources pertains to the poems not concerned with music. Walter Arndt, ed. and trans., *Alexander Pushkin: Collected Narrative and Lyrical Poetry*; Neal Ascherson, *Black Sea*; Peter Green, trans. Ovid: *The Poems of Exile*; Clarence Brown and W.S. Merwin, trans., Osip Mandelstam, 'Tristia'; Yon Barna, *Eisenstein* ('Sadnesses: Black Seas'). Christopher Bamford, ed., *The Noble Traveller: The Life and Writings of O.V. de L. Milosz*: John Peck, trans., O.V. de L. Milosz, 'Quand Elle Viendra . . .' ('Geneva Pension'). Wilbur F. Hinnman, *The Story of the Sherman Brigade* ('Ohio Forbears'). Peter Jay, trans., *The Song of Songs* ('Variations on *The Song of Songs*'); William Carlos Williams, 'The Turtle' ('Letter to an Unborn Grandson').

III

Ernest Hemingway, the novels, stories and *A Moveable Feast*; Carlos Baker, *Ernest Hemingway: A Life Story*; Michael Reynolds, the five volumes of his Hemingway biography: *The Young Hemingway, The Paris Years, The Homecoming, Hemingway in the 1930s, Hemingway: The Final Years*. Constance Cappel, *Hemingway in Michigan*; Dorothy Munson Krenrigh, *Muhqua Nebis: Legends of Walloon Lake* ('Swell').

From *Kedging*

I: Post-Anecdotal
Andre Gide, *If It Die: An Autobiography* ('Post-Anecdotal'). John Matthias, 'Kedging in Time,' 'Kedging in "Kedging in Time,"' *Oxford English Dictionary* ('Kedging'). Ezra Pound, 'Prefatory Note to "The Complete Poetical Works of T.E. Hulme"', *Personae*; Geoffrey Hill, 'Genesis' ('Hoosier Horologe'). Solomon Volkov, 'The ABCs of Shnittke,' liner notes for Kronos Quartet, *The Complete String Quartets of Alfred Schnittke* ('Polystylistics'). Sir Walter Ralegh, 'What Is Our Life?' ('Not Will Kempe'). Ingemar Bergman, *Smultronstället, Four Screenplays*; Göran Printz-Påhlson, *Säg Minns Du Skeppet Refanut? Samlade dikter 1950-1983* ('Smultronstället'). Oscar Williams, *A Pocket Book of Modern Verse* ("Oscar"). Charles Baudelaire, 'Spleen' I–IV; Ezra Pound, 'Hugh Selwyn Mauberley' ('Red Root's Spleen'). Ian Watt, *Essays on Conrad*, David Lean, 'The Bridge over the River Kwai'

('Another Movie, Colonel B.'). Stanley Weintraub, *Whistler: A Biography*; Ezra Pound, 'To Whistler, American' ('Arrangement in Gray and Black'). John Gardner and John Mair, *Gilgamesh: Translated from the Sin Leqi Unninni Version* ('Column I, Tablet XIII'). Given the topicality, along with the tragic nature of circumstances leading to this allusive but not impersonal poem, I include the following extended note, originally written for an anthology. Paralleling a similar note to '26 June 1381/1977' in volume I of my *Collected Shorter Poems*, it also suggests why I have limited these notes almost entirely to bibliography. Adequate annotation, though perhaps desirable, is impossible in a book of this length, or perhaps any book:

> I don't remember where I was when news began to come in about the bombing of the United Nations Baghdad office at the Kanal Hotel on August 19, 2003, but it was clear by the next day that Sergio Vieira de Mello, the top UN envoy in Iraq and perhaps heir apparent for the position of UN Secretary General, had died after spending three hours trying to direct rescue efforts from his cell phone. Eventually, reports began to arrive on the news media about "a man called Gil" who had evidently been the only person rescued from de Mello's part of the building, and who might just possibly survive. By the time my wife got home from work, she knew that "Gil" was Gilburt Loescher, our long-time University of Notre Dame colleague and next-door neighbor, who had recently taken early retirement to live in Oxford and work for the Institute for Strategic Studies. When my wife walked in the door, looking shattered, she said, "Gil Loescher was badly injured in Baghdad. Both of his legs had to be amputated in order to free him from the rubble."
>
> If there was a trouble spot in the world, we were never surprised to hear that Gil had been there or was on his way. At Notre Dame he worked at the Kroc Institute for International Peace and was a fellow of the Kellogg Institute for International Studies. His academic interest and, more importantly, his human calling had to do with refugees. He had probably done humanitarian work in half the refugee camps in the world. When he was at his desk, he wrote books like his official history of the U.N. High Commission on Refugees, but he was more likely to be on a plane than at his desk. He had flown to Baghdad "to assess the human cost of the war and occupation," and he was planning to report his findings to the U.N. He himself became part of the human cost of the war and occupation within 24 hours of arriving.
>
> One does not immediately sit down and write a poem on hearing that a friend has been blown up in a war and may not survive. All of Gil's friends—and they come from all over the

world—did what friends try to do in situations like this: give whatever comfort they can from whatever distance by whatever means. Gil's wife and daughters were flown to Germany where Gil was taken for emergency surgery and a long period of recovery. When he was able to write about it himself, this is what he said.

"On our arrival, we went straightaway to the third floor office of Sergio Vieria de Mello, the U.N. envoy to Iraq. At exactly the same time, a cement truck driven by a suicide bomber and loaded with explosives was circling the compound, looking for a way in. As I exchanged greetings with Sergio and with several members of his staff, the suicide attacker was able to turn into the space directly under Sergio's office and detonate his bomb. The deafening explosion collapsed the ceiling of the third floor upon us and crushed to death several of the people in the room. Others were killed or severely injured when the bomb shattered the windows of the building, sending fragments flying everywhere. The bomb killed Arthur Helton and 21 others and left 150 people wounded. I lost both my legs above the knees, severely damaged my right hand and suffered numerous shrapnel wounds. I lay trapped, hanging by my ruined legs that were caught between the floor and the collapsed ceiling of Sergio's office. Later I was to learn that I didn't bleed to death because I was hanging upside down."

Eventually I felt compelled to write something. As part of a generation responsible for glib and self-important political poems during the period of the Viet Nam war, I hesitate to write any longer what is generally considered to be "political poetry." Nonetheless, I couldn't get two things out of my mind: That Gil somehow rhymed with Gilgamesh, hero of the great Mesopotamian epic, and that his life had been saved because he hung upside down in the air. When the Loeschers were still living next door, Gil's wife Ann and I had tried for some time to hang a bird feeder from a wire strung between our two houses. In the end, we found it worked better hanging upside down. Gil found this funny, laughing at us as he looked up from the book he was reading in his garden.

There are only XII tablets in *Gilgamesh*, most in fragments. My fragment is therefore from apocryphal tablet XIII. *Gilgamesh* is about a great friendship, about the search for immortality, about many other things. Enkidu is the friend. Humbaba is a monster. A late version of the poem was first written down by Sin-leqi-unninni. It is the one usually followed in translations. My poem is, of course, achingly inadequate. The important thing is that Gil survived and continues to do his work, both for the living and in memory of those who did not survive.

Walter Davis, *The Works of Thomas Campion*; Cornelius Eady, 'Muddy Waters & the Chicago Blues' ('Walter's House'). Wallace Stevens, 'Anecdote of the Jar' ('The Large Iron Saucepan'). John Berryman, *The Dream Songs*, 385, John Matthias, *Crossing* and *Collected Shorter Poems*, vol. I, 'Poem for Cynouai' ('Missing Cynouai').

II: The Memoirists
Lorenzo da Ponte, *Memoirs* ('The Grocer'). Edward John Trelawny, *Records of Shelley, Byron and the Author* ('The Pirate'). Frederick Rolfe, Baron Corvo, *The Desire and Pursuit of the Whole* ('The Gondolier'). Celeste Albaret, *Monsieur Proust* ('The Housekeeper'). Vernon Duke, *Passport to Paris* ('Epilogue: Four Seasons of Vladimir Dukelsky').

## *The HIJ* and Other Poems

I
'Fragment: At the Tomb of Henry Howard,' designated 'Last of the East Anglian Poems, left unfinished, April, 1995.' *Collected Shorter Poems*, Vol. I, and *Collected Longer Poems* contain many pieces written in and/or about the East Anglian region of Britain. A few stragglers looking back to periods in the 1970s and early 80s when I lived in Suffolk and Cambridge survive in the period—1995–2011—covered by this book. *The Odyssey*, Book III; Roberto Calasso, *The Marriage of Cadmus and Harmony* ('Artemis, Aging ...').

II
Heinrich Heine, 'Der Doppelgänger' ('The Double: After Heine'). Aeschylus, *Agamemnon*; Euripides, *Iphigenia in Aulis*; George Seferis, 'Euripides the Athenian,' ('After George Seferis'). Horace, *Satires* I, 6 ('After Horae'). Sophocles, *The Three Theban Plays*, Trans. with Introduction and Notes by Robert Fagles ('Kolonos Hippios'). Aren Maeir, *Biblical Archaeology Review*, May–June, 2008; 1 *Samuel* 6 ('Biblical Archaeology'). D.H. Lawrence, *Etruscan Places*; Jacques Heurgon, *Daily Life of the Etruscans* ('Lorenzo England Clan Alvis Lupu XLV'). Ezra Pound, *The Pisan Cantos*; Barbara Guest, *Herself Defined: The Poet H.D. And Her World*; F. Scott Fitzgerald, *Tender is the Night* and *The Last Tycoon*; Jeffrey Meyers, *Scott Fitzgerald*; Tom Dardis, *Some Time in the Sun* ('Modernatro Pizzicato' and 'Their Flims'). Paul Mariani, *William Carlos Williams*; Robin D.G. Kelley, *Thelonious Monk: The Life and Times of an American Original*; William Carlos Williams, 'Complaint' ('The Baronesses'). Charles Olson, *The Maximus Poems*, 'Letters' 1-7 and 'The Songs of Maximus'; Edward Dorn, 'From Gloucester Out'; Hilda Morley, *What Are Winds & What Are Waters*; Thomas Wolfe, *Look Homeward, Angel*; Elizabeth Nowell, *Thomas Wolfe: A Biography* ('Asheville Out').

III
Dana Hedgpeth, Lisa Rein, and Jonathan O'Connell, 'In St. Elizabeths Project, Opportunities for Many,' *The Washington Post*, April 26, 2010; James Bamford, *The Shadow Factory* ('When They Sent Him Back'). Miscellaneous papers, Göran Printz-Påhlson collection, Lund University archives ('Interlinear Dialogue with a Poem Found with Letters from Göran Printz-Påhlson'). Personal correspondence from Guy Davenport ('Postcards from the Sofa').

IV
Robert Harris, *Pompeii*; John Dryden, *Aureng-Zebe* ('The Plumber'). Paul Muldoon, 'The Sightseers' ('Not Quite'). Academy Award Night, 2011: The reference to stuttering is to Colin Firth's performance in *The King's Speech* ('For an Old Actor Exploited at the Awards'). W.B. Yeats, 'To a Friend Whose Work Has Come to Nothing' ('To a Fraud Whose Work Has Come to Be Canonical'). Jesper Svenbro, *Three-toed Gull: Selected Poems*, trans. John Matthias and Lars-Håkan Svensson; Elizabeth Bishop, 'Santarém' ('The Cotranslator's Dilemma' and 'Stalin as Wolf'). John Matthias and Göran Printz-Påhlson, *Contemporary Swedish Poetry* ('Göran Printz-Påhlson: Two Poems').

V: The HIJ
*Oxford English Dictionary* on line and related Internet links ('The HIJ').

§

Readers who are acquainted with my *New Selected Poems* (Salt, 2004) may remember that I there stated a preference for representing both longer and shorter poems in the same volume. In the case of what will to be a *Collected Poems* in three volumes, I find that I have changed my mind. Given the chronological development of my work over forty years, it makes most sense at present to frame a single volume of longer poems with two volumes of shorter poems, the first collecting work from 1963–1994, and the second work from 1995–2011, including previously unpublished poems. The present volume of shorter poems, chronologically the most recent, is published first in order to make new poems available now rather than later. The one-volume *Collected Longer Poems* will follow, and then the 1963–1994 volume of *Collected Shorter Poems*.

The few exceptions to chronological order in this volume are not significant enough to bother anyone who wants to think of it as an historical record of some kind. Any patterns, of course, will become clearer when these poems can be read alongside work to appear in the next two books.

J.M., 15 July 2011

www.ingramcontent.com/pod-product-compliance
Lightning Source LLC
Chambersburg PA
CBHW032125160426
43197CB00008B/522